"Someone has said that life has two great n
the second is the moment we discover wh
must be understood in light of the ways v
follow Christ as Lord, the best way to do s
Sister, Rev. Dr. Arnetta McNeese Bailey, has done a wonderful job of introducing us to Bible characters and allowing us to see and meet ourselves in their lives, all while inviting us into her own life and journey. In so many ways this book becomes like the Bible—a mirror that allows us to see ourselves—and that is a blessing. This book is an eye-opener, a page-turner, and a life changer. Be blessed by it."

—Bishop Timothy J. Clarke, Author of *Bind Up Your Broken Heart*

"*It's Not In Vain* brings to life the stories of twelve women in the Bible, connecting their challenges with Dr. Arnetta Bailey's own testimony of trauma and triumph. The result is a treasure trove of lessons in personal formation for vocation in ministry. Her legacy of devoted discipleship and courageous leadership as CEO of a global Christian women's organization shines through on every page!"

—Cheryl J. Sanders, Author of *Ministry at the Margins*, *Saints in Exile*, and *Empowerment Ethics for a Liberated People*

"This book is a compelling read for anyone seeking to follow the call of God. The author convincingly reminds us that our past choices may inform our future but do not define it. With great vulnerability, Dr. Bailey allows past and future friends a glimpse into her personal and professional life to discover how strengths and weaknesses can be used to the glory of God. As a master teacher, she allows the echo of female voices in the Old and New Testaments to reverberate with a new generation. While the book is written with her sisters of the faith in mind, it would be a mistake for Reverend Bailey's spiritual brothers to miss these important alpha and omega truths of a life of faithful service. I recommend *It's Not in Vain* for individuals and groups desiring to better understand the call of God on the lives of ordinary people."

—David Sebastian, Dean Emeritus, Minister at Large, Anderson University, Anderson, Indiana

"My soul longs to hear from authentic, godly people who aren't perfect, but who are constantly aligning their hearts, lives, and minds with Christ and his Word. There are so many voices, so many options, so many demands and expectations. What a joy to sit with a sister at the table of fellowship and hear from her heart how God is blessing, healing, and calling her into the next season of life and ministry. Thank you, Arnetta, for your faithfulness and for sharing your journey with other hungry souls!"

—Jeannette Flynn, Executive Director of Leadership Focus, Church of God Ministries

Published by Warner Press, Inc.

Requests for information should be sent to:

Warner Press, Inc.
PO Box 2499
Anderson, IN 46018-2499

warnerpress.org

Editor: Elizabeth Flinn
Cover Design: Curtis Corzine
Layout Design: Katie Miller

ISBN: 9781684343416 (Soft Cover)

ISBN: 9781684343423 (E-Pub)

Printed in the United States of America.

TABLE OF CONTENTS

ACKNOWLEDGEMENTS

To my children—Markus, Jamal, Merleynn, and their spouses, Shatika and Jermaine—every step of the way you have told me to keep going. Thank you for permission to share parts of your story and for your unconditional love and support. There is nothing I value more than being a mom; after God, you are my priority and delight.

To my parents—Elder Dr. Timmie McNeese and Rev. Priscilla D. McNeese—before there were any other influences in my head, God blessed me with clear memories of your voices. Thank you for never failing to speak purpose into my life and the many ways you modeled servant leadership before me. Oma Jean McNeese, thank you for providing objectivity when things got cloudy. To my aunt, Vannetta Greene, thank you for being the best surrogate mother, cheerleader, traveling companion, and giver of unconditional love; I honor you always.

To my siblings—Barbara (Bobbi), Marvin, Mose, Timi (TD), Wes, Saundra, and the two God called home, Merle and Timothy—thank you for being the wind beneath my wings. I never had to look outside to others to see what excellence, creativity, commitment, success, or a follower of Christ looked like. You gave me the blueprint to follow and a standard to live up to. Thank you for always being my "big brothers and sisters" and for supporting and encouraging me to find my own path.

Thank you to the wonderful women I have had the pleasure of serving on staff with down through the years. However, the last team—Melanie Thigpen, Gretchen Smith, Karen Sayre, Lori Dixon, Darlene McGough, Juanita Swift, and Jan Edwards—have been the ones ordained by God to help me finish the last leg of this journey and move confidently into the next season of ministry.

To the Christian Women Connection Board of Directors and Council—thank you for the freedom and flexibility given to me to complete this book. The calls, e-mails, and gentle prodding to keep writing blessed me in ways you cannot imagine.

Rev. Marilyn Lambe—thank you for showing me how to lead, for reminding me that it all began with a solid prayer life, and for never asking those you serve with to do something you are not willing to do yourself.

Rev. L. Pearl Shields—thanks for your prophetic words thirty years ago and for holding me accountable.

I have been blessed to have several "Pauls" in my life. Pastor Ron Fowler—thanks for dreaming for me. Pastor Eustace Rawlings and Pastor Art Leftridge—thanks for recognizing and encouraging the call.

Vondie Boykin, Cynthia Thomas, Michelle Paige, Naomi Bryant, Felecia Smith, Elsa Johnson-Bass, Valerie Johnson, and Pamela Graves—thank you for "keeping it real."

To the awesome group of ladies who I consider my Dream Team—you have literally helped me every step of the way to make the dream of writing this book become a reality: Melanie Thigpen, Mary Stephens, Erin Lantz, and Jewel Williams. From where to begin, how to identify my style of writing, editing, critiquing, and advising, you labored with me non-stop. Thank you for your tireless efforts and never saying *no* when I sent those late-night e-mails with a revision.

PREFACE

Why the need for another women's Bible study and devotional? The market is already saturated with wonderful resources from which to choose. So, what will make this book stand out? That question will only be satisfied at the completion of this book—if your response is that *reading this book was not in vain.* Read with an open heart and mind so that God can speak to you through the pages as you journey with Mary, Hannah, Deborah, and me. May each story help you realize and respond to your significance and standing before God.

This book is not about one set of events but a lifetime of events—experiences from my ordinary life being used by God to do what I classify as extraordinary things. It is the honest story of my struggles, my inability to see my self-worth, my doubts, and the precious moments of clarity when I sensed the unfailing presence of God's love and care in my life.

I am not a well-known speaker with an identifiable name in the broader Christian arena. Outside of the affiliation of my religious community, I am not on anyone's radar. Yet, God used me to travel the world and to share his gospel. Someone once described me as not being a little fish in a big pond but a big fish in a little pond. I'm not sure whether this was intended as a compliment, but it did describe my pilgrimage to serve in national ministries within my faith communion.

This book is a compilation of stories, biblical and personal, of choosing to live victorious and not as a victim. That choice was not easy. I had to learn to live through my hurts, disappointments, and failures in a public arena, all the while serving with an authentic smile. I chose joy when I wanted to go home and be sad, yet was honest that there were days when I was sad and alone and felt hopeless. *It's Not in Vain* is a telling of how I used those moments of despair as teachable moments. I used those times as object lessons on what to do next time or how to prevent a next time from occurring.

I love the study of biblical characters—not just women, but all the narratives in the Bible have often peaked my curiosity. I wanted to take a closer look into the depths of their stories. The challenge for me was which women I would use for this book and why. What stories did I want to tell and what was the best way to frame those stories and stay true to the Scriptures? Eve taught me there is always more to the story. Don't stop at the mistake a person makes; we serve a God of restoration and reconciliation.

Deborah's life was a clear message of how we need each other; God never intended for us to go it alone. The story of the woman with the alabaster jar is a message to all women, especially those who think they have less to offer—just do what you can! What God has given you, if given back to him, just may touch lives on the other side of the world.

It's Not in Vain is not an autobiography. Who would benefit from a book by an unknown "fish" in a small pond? I believe everyone can. "Sisters, think of what you were when you were called. Not many of you were wise by human standards; not many were influential; not many were of noble birth. But God chose the foolish things of the world to shame the wise; God chose the weak things of the world to shame the strong. God chose the lowly things of this world and the despised things—and the things that are not—to nullify the things that are" (1 Corinthians 1:26–28).

FOREWORD

It was on a beautiful afternoon while I was walking outdoors in the sun that I answered the phone to what would turn out to be one of the most beautiful souls with whom I had ever talked. That beautiful soul was Rev. Dr. Arnetta McNeese Bailey. She began to share her life story with me, and I felt comfortable sharing my life story with her. Our shared passion for Jesus, the Church of God, the empowerment of women, growing leaders, and the desire to help the marginalized in our world formed an immediate kindred bond. What struck me the most was Dr. Arnetta's seldom-found combination of confidence and humility. One of those traits did not cancel out the other one, but a beautiful woven combination of these two traits compelled me to learn more about who she was. Dr. Arnetta has served Christian Women Connection since 2002. She has also served the church extensively as a board member of Children of Promise, the Executive Leadership Strategic Planning Committee, the Reconciliation Task Force, and the Circle of Missions Committee. She is the founder and executive director of Priscilla's Lost and Found as well as other ministries.

Being a woman in ministry myself and having the opportunity to minister worldwide, Dr. Arnetta quickly became a valued colleague and colaborer in the work of the gospel. In this terrific book, *It's Not in Vain,* Dr. Arnetta exquisitely shows how women from the very beginning of time have been at the heart of God. She also helps us understand the value he has placed on women and how women are essential to his purposes and plans for humanity. *It's Not in Vain* looks at twelve women from the Scriptures, showing us how our lives can be a part of a larger and magnificent tapestry of divine design. Dr. Arnetta has an authenticity that is not only refreshing but empowering. Her capacity to tell a story, both personal and biblical, is captivating and riveting.

Dr. Arnetta shows through women's lives in both the Old and New Testaments that a surrendered life is a choice and that the surrendered life is also sacred. Nothing is haphazard to God. He will not waste a single experience, a single tear, a single hurt, a single loss, or a single failure in our lives. He will use it all to help us live up to and beyond our potential. One of the most significant points that *It's Not in Vain* makes is that our future is greater than our sin. "Now take off the veil and be known," Dr. Arnetta writes, and "live beyond the labels and expect the remarkable."

If you are a woman who has limiting beliefs that are holding you back, read *It's Not in Vain* and find the freedom that is yours in Christ. If you are a woman held back by fear and inadequacies, read *It's Not in Vain* and experience God's presence as you live your life at the "Red Sea" moments of miracles. If you are a woman desiring a voice that is vibrant, strong, and victorious, read *It's Not in Vain* and find the power and freedom of your voice. If you are a woman who longs for a larger footprint of ministry influence for the kingdom, read *It's Not in Vain* and find the "sky's the limit" possibilities. Or if you are a woman who wants to be closer to Jesus, read *It's Not in Vain* and find an intimacy with Christ that never disappoints.

When I read this book, I saw Jesus more clearly, sensed a closeness with the women of the Scriptures, and even with you, the reader. Dr. Arnetta reminds us that we are of immense value to God and his purposes and plan for the world. As a sisterhood, we will go forward arm-in-arm with an uncommon unity, with each other and with our sisters in Scripture, to live our lives free, vibrant, and with power. I passionately encourage you to read *It's Not in Vain.*

Lori Salierno Maldonado, D.Min.

INTRODUCTION

The nudge to write this book came in 2005. It was birthed from countless hours wasted on the *what-if* and the *why-did-this-happen-to-me* questions. On the night before I was to be in meetings that would decide the biggest ministry assignment I had ever been given, I finally put pen to paper and began to record my thoughts.

It was October 1, 2007, and I was to be ratified as executive director of the Women of the Church of God the next day, but I was on a do-not-travel order from my doctor. Thoughts flooded my mind, and each one was beyond my control. *God, how can this happen; what will happen if I am not there? Lord, I need to be there. Surely this ratification will not happen if I am too sick to be in attendance! How and why would they have confidence in my ability to lead? I need to be there to stand and share my vision.* The only choice I had control of that day was how I would wait. Would I surrender to fear of the unknown, or would I exercise my faith as I sat alone in my family room waiting for the call that would change the course of my ministry?

What if? and *Why did this happen to me?* are questions that everyone has asked. The question is not the problem; it's the unproductive moments that we spend in worry and regret that rob us of our joy and peace. There is too much grieving happening rather than receiving the gift of God in Christ Jesus. Psalm 139:16 says, "Your eyes saw my unformed body; all the days ordained for me were written in your book before one of them came to be." I had to stop being anxious about completing this book. Why? Because as time passed, I recognized there were more lessons to be taught, more life to experience, and more love to behold. Rest assured, everything that has happened in my life and yours is not in vain.

In the latter part of 2001, I was encouraged by Rev. Dr. Ronald J. Fowler and Bishop Timothy J. Clarke to apply for the job of ministry coordinator at Women of the Church of God, and I resisted, not once but on several occasions. I did not want to be pigeonholed into what I perceived as a box relegated to women's day and women's ministry only. How limited my view of God was! After I began serving, I totally and completely fell in love with every aspect of women's ministry. It has been an honor to inspire, empower, encourage, and equip women for Kingdom service. This new phase of my life has allowed me to mentor and encourage the next generation of leaders, who just happen to be women. Oh my, Church of God, look out! They are bold, fierce, and passionate visionaries and social-justice activists and, even more importantly, lovers of God and his church.

It is now 2021, and I am finally completing this book. The backdrop is very different. The COVID-19 pandemic has swept the land, and we have no control over our schedules or futures. We seek to observe the stay-in-place orders to help ensure that our families stay free of the virus. And now, I am planning my retirement from that assignment that began in 2007. Thirteen years later, God has shown me much and allowed me to serve as executive director of Christian Women Connection, formerly Women of the Church of God. My love and respect for this ministry and the opportunities that it has afforded me are beyond measure. I had so many plans for this final year of service. I had plotted and calculated what I would do each month to finish strong. Yet, here I sit again alone in my office waiting, understanding with an awareness that I did not possess early in ministry that it is okay to not be in control. It is comforting to know that I don't have to be. Because God is! Certain facts of my future and the course of my ministry are about to change, yet I have peace—a peace born out of every experience, hurt, disappointment, success, and failure. All of it was necessary for the next phase of the journey. Nothing was in vain.

May all my studies, early mornings, and late nights in prayer and preparation bring God glory. May it all serve to help others, my sisters in particular, better understand, glean from, and reflect on the moments of their lives and realize *it was not in vain!*

When I began writing this book, I tried to shy away from the use of women's narratives as examples. However, I found that I would miss so much of the journey if I did not use women and their life stories to show that God most certainly had women at the heart of his plan and in his heart. In their stories we find wisdom, ability, and self-worth. I have been blessed to preach, teach, and live so many of their life lessons. Join me as I journey from the beginning when God created Adam and Eve. I have found, and hope you will discover again and again, the value God placed on his daughters and how he brought full emancipation to women.

PART 1

God's Plan

CHAPTER 1

God's Plan from the Beginning

In him we were also chosen, having been predestined according to the plan of him who works out everything in conformity with the purpose of his will.
—Ephesians 1:11

Here Paul was saying, to those who have acted in response to their chosenness, that God's plan is being manifested in our lives according to his will. Bring together all the things you know about God's character and his great love for you; settle in the knowledge that his plan for us is truly for good and never for evil.

Looking back at my life's threads and my prayers, I realized how often I had asked God to remove hard times from my life. These are unrealistic expectations, but too often they are our prayers. I hope to convey in this book that we should cease those prayers. Hard places are opportunities for growth, and they are beneficial. We grow in the valleys, in the depths of our pain. Everyone would rather not go through the hurt, pain, struggle, strife, and disease of life. But remember, God is at work in our life's struggles, according to his plan.

So began my journey of reflection that everything I have experienced had purpose, woven together for a greater plan. I have come to accept, not enjoy, bad things that happen. Life is complicated and sometimes messy, but I never doubt that God knows and that he foreknew. Everything has to yield, to conform to the counsel of his will.

Eve: The Mother of All Who Lived

Genesis 1—3

Often, when we hear sermons and teachings on Eve, they fall painfully short of this woman's fullness—the woman whom Adam named Eve, which means *life-giving*. Commentaries and viewpoints of Eve's life focus solely on her mistake and often fail to mention or remind the reader that she was still made in God's image and likeness. One writer describes Eve's story as pathetic. Oh, how I dare to differ. *Pathetic* would be an apt description if her life were one-dimensional. Yet there are so many facets to this woman. God's plan for redemption is one.

Surely there has to be more to Eve than her mistake, her sin. If her narrative is so void of depth and substance, then we are left to think there was no plan for Eve's life beyond the sin brought into the world. We know that to be untrue. Eve's life, her influence, was much more than her part in the fall. I will not trivialize this event or minimize its effect on humankind, but it is not the whole story.

Eve was more than her sin, and she rose above it. Writers and commentaries may tend to overlook these details, but Scripture does not. Eve could have easily stopped at *What if?* and *Why me, Lord?* but it would have been an unproductive exercise. This insightful woman regrouped and once again focused on what was important: her relationship with God and her family. Her choice to listen to Satan was foolish and carried with it great consequences. Her life went from a peaceful existence in the garden of Eden to separation from God. The long walks with God in the coolness of the evenings were over. Adam became a laborer, and she would suffer pain during her privileged moment of bringing another life into this world. Yet, that was not the end of the story.

Let me document just a few contributions of Eve, a woman of distinction with many firsts to her credit. Eve was the first woman on this earth; she was something to behold in her physical appearance. "Wo-man" was the way Adam described her. Eve was created, formed, and designed specifically to be a helpmate for Adam. Her existence completed Adam. She was an influencer. Eve was a fashion designer; she was the first mother, the first to lose one child to death and another to discontent. She was the first person by words and actions to recognize that God is always in pursuit of us, reconciling us to himself, seeking a relationship with us. "Adam made love to his wife again, and she gave birth to a son and named him Seth, saying, 'God has granted me another child in place of Abel, since Cain killed him' " (Genesis 4:25).

We speak Eve's name, celebrate her life, and bemoan her choices, yet we appreciate the examples she left for us to follow. Eve may not have known how her life choice would affect humankind for all eternity, but one thing is certain: she didn't give up or give in. She kept living. Eve lived the first words spoken over life, the word of God—*she was made in God's image and likeness.* She didn't slip away into obscurity; she modeled strength and fortitude.

There will be many words spoken to you, about you, and over you. If you must believe anything, believe the first words spoken by God on your behalf: You are made in his image, be fruitful and multiply; we have dominion, and we are very good. Follow that plan, use this blueprint. Eve did.

Reflection

What are a few lessons we can glean from the mother of all living people? In the beginning, God planned to be in relationship with us and provide a way to reconcile us back to himself. We can do nothing to erase the choices we made in the past, but they most certainly do not define our future. Inform yes, but not define.

We are *rare*! We are unique creations of God. There is only one you. We are unusually good and remarkable. I heard a young woman preaching a sermon once say, "On your worst day, no one can beat you at being you." Those words gave me life, a new perspective.

Paul said in Ephesians 2:10, "For we are God's handiwork, created in Christ Jesus to do good works, which God prepared in advance for us to do." God created and formed us; he breathed the breath of life into us. No one can alter God's plan for our lives. He created us in Christ Jesus, made us in his image and his likeness. He called each one of us; it is not an exclusive club for popular people only. This work is for all humankind to participate in, to take ownership and stewardship over. This work has been uniquely designed for us.

Too often, we focus on what we cannot do. Ephesians 2:10 is empowering because it allows us to see that we each have an assignment. There is a task, a ministry, an opportunity uniquely designed for you. It is tailor-made for your skill set, your personality, and your touch. Expect to have a few mishaps along the way because life is not perfect. (I didn't say expect to sin, no license here, I said *mishaps*.) However, don't let those situations cause you to doubt yourself or doubt God.

You, dear sister, are *rare*. Nothing you have done or will do will change how God sees you. You are fearfully and wonderfully made.

To know that we are God's handiwork alone is affirming, but it doesn't end there. Paul said, "which God prepared in advance" (Ephesians 2:10). My sister, since it is already written, recorded, ordained, written in his book before we even came to be, and purposed for us to do, stop fretting.

God has already prepared in advance the outcome. (We win!) We can either focus on how big the assignment is or focus on how majestic God is. We can fret and live in doubt, or declare, "I can do all things." We can recite our lack of resources, income, or experience. Or we can believe God has prepared in advance for us to succeed. We have been predestined, chosen to win. We succeed because we are his rare creation.

Eve dealt with the *reality* of her sin. There are consequences to the choices we make, but the story is still being written. It is not the end. God works out everything: setbacks, disappointments, tests and trials, closed doors, *everything*.

I grew up in the 1960s, when we jumped rope at recess. Those fifteen-to-twenty-minute breaks we received twice a day to go out on the playground helped release all that energy. If you jumped the rope and didn't like how the person "turned the rope," you could call a do-over. A mistake was made, and it would provide a second chance. Unfortunately, life doesn't allow many do-overs. Wouldn't it be wonderful if, for every anxious moment, mistake, bad decision, misdeed, or oversight we missed along the way, we could simply say, "Do-over!" Wouldn't it be wonderful if we could have our jubilee: all our debts cancelled, sins forgiven, and property returned! Unfortunately, there are no do-overs, but they are not necessary with Christ Jesus. God offers us one better: his unfailing love and grace that is sufficient, and his willingness to cast our sins into the depths of the sea! If God can forgive us, why can't we forgive ourselves? If he says, "Before I formed you in the womb I knew you...I set you apart" (Jeremiah 1:5), then rest assured, everything that has happened to you in your life and from this day forward was not in vain.

Even in Eve's stumbling, she didn't attempt to shy away from or ignore the consequences of her choice. She lived her reality and continued to respond appropriately to life's circumstances. She continued to be a helpmate for Adam and was called to be a mother. She loved with a mother's heart. When Cain killed Abel, I am sure she grieved as one would expect. However, at some point, this mother arose from her grief. She bore another son and, in the process, acknowledged the longsuffering love of God: "She…named him Seth, saying, 'God has granted me another child' " (Genesis 4:25). God did not change her role, he called her to be a mother.

Live your truth, no matter how muddy or complicated it may be! Own it, but do not let it cripple or define you. People want to know that you are authentic. Everyone is not required to share the details of their struggles, sins, or mistakes. But I promise you your story has a healing balm for another sister. I remember when I found out that there was healing in my testimony. God kept putting me in positions and situations where I felt led to share. I was always afraid of others' judgment until I realized the freedom I felt when I shared. I don't celebrate sin; I celebrate the Son! We overcome "by the blood of the Lamb and by the word of [our] testimony" (Revelation 12:11). Don't let the enemy or others hold you hostage to your past. There are people out there waiting to hear that they, too, can make it. Someone needs to know that all the things she lived through has brought her to her today; it was not in vain.

If we don't deal with it, we will continuously be running from it. Eve said that God had granted her another son, another chance, another opportunity to live out his calling on her life. Because Eve didn't shy away from her sin or the sin of her family, it was during the time of Seth, the father of Enosh, that people began to call on the name of the Lord. God was working on Eve's behalf even during her darkest hours. Imagine the pain of a mother having to endure the death of a child. And, if that wasn't hard enough on its own, that death was at the hand of his sibling. What can one say? How do you offer comfort? How can one make sense of this tragedy? There are times when we don't have answers to the difficult questions, but we trust in God, who is all-knowing and loving.

In Eve's grief, God brought *restoration*. There is no doubt that there was divine communication with God for Eve to name this child Seth, the son to replace Abel and the one through which the Messiah would come.

From the beginning, God was at work in all things: "For those God foreknew he also predestined" (Romans 8:29).

I am the daughter of pastors; both my parents served in pastoral roles. My dad served for over fifty years. However, that was not the path I chose. I believed there was a God, but giving my life to him was not the road I traveled at first. Yet, there was something on the inside that kept wooing me. I wandered far away from God, but I realize now that God's hand was always protecting me.

Like Eve, I chose to listen to the enemy's voice only to be disappointed time after time. I tried to fit in, but God's plan for my life finally spoke louder than my desire to sin. I remember once, when I was trying to be like the other girls, God used a friendly voice to remind me, "Netta, don't do that; that is not who you are." Those words rang in my spirit for years until I surrendered my heart to the Lord.

I have sinned and have lived with the consequences of those sins. I, like so many of you, have lived with and endured suffering out of my control, even the loss of a child. And if that were not painful enough, at the same time I lost the ability to bear children. However, God brought restoration into my life. He restored my soul and blessed me with two amazing sons who bring me joy daily and a niece who has loved me and allowed me the privilege to mother her. God replaced some things taken from me, but more importantly, he brought revival into my heart. I remember the day when my home began to call upon the name of the Lord.

Conclusion

Are you convinced God has a plan for your life? I mean, *truly* convinced? After the message has grown dim and the book has been placed back on the shelf, have you held on to the certainty that in the great scheme of things you too were planned? Before you were formed, God knew you; he set you apart. As God was creating the earth, setting the stars in place, and forming Adam and Eve, you too were on his mind. It has taken a lot for me to grasp that thought in its entirety because we are finite. We are limited in our scope and abilities. No matter how great we are at multi-tasking and juggling family matters, we seldom plan beyond two generations. But God's plans are infinite.

Whatever odds may seem to be against you, whether it be an unfortunate beginning, missteps along the way, or a current situation of despair, God is not unaware. "Many are the afflictions of the righteous: but the LORD delivereth him out of them all" (Psalm 34:19, KJV).

My dear sister, whatever has happened to you or because of you, God will never stop working on your behalf.

Greater is he that is in you than anything you will face in this world.

Questions for Reflection

1. How has God shown glimpses of his plan for you despite your past mistakes?
2. What part of God's plan do you feel may have been paused, like an unfinished book placed back on a shelf?
3. Write down and share three hopes that you want to be included regarding God's plan for your life. Or write down three things that you feel are against you, and dream how these things could be working *for* you.

CHAPTER 2

God's Plan Includes You

For all of you who were baptized into Christ have clothed yourselves with Christ. There is neither Jew nor Gentile, neither slave nor free, nor is there male and female, for you are all one in Christ Jesus. If you belong to Christ, then you are Abraham's seed, and heirs according to the promise.
—Galatians 3:27–29

Paul was addressing the Gentiles here, but he could have used any people group as an example. The message would have been the same: if we are in Christ, we are Abraham's seed, and the promise includes us. All Christians, followers of Christ, are heirs to the promise. No matter the standing, sex, or race, God involved every one of us. By faith in Christ Jesus, God has bequeathed on us eternal blessings of grace.

Sometimes it takes longer for some to grasp this reality. Those who take hold of God's plan early seem to walk with more confidence. Those who struggle to accept the worthiness of inclusion tend to believe their giftedness is lacking or that others must be superior to what they have when, in reality, this is not the case. There are no exceptions or inequities in Christ; our faith and trust in God make the difference.

I remember the times clearly when I wondered if I was included, long before the thought of ministry. It began as early as giftings within my family. I was blessed to be born into an amazingly gifted family. My siblings are truly my first and always heroes. They excelled at everything they touched. I was the youngest in my family and accustomed to them making things easier for me, but it didn't help my self-esteem. For a very long time, I felt inferior.

It wasn't that God had not included me; I didn't think I could live up to their standards, so as a result, I didn't try hard. It wasn't until I reached high school that I met two teachers who happened to be my older siblings' classmates. Edna Farmer and Doris Massenberg weren't having it. They knew the potential I had on the inside (what they perceived as my birthright) and demanded that I worked up to that potential. They encouraged me, pushed me, and refused to let me accept ordinary. They were relentless until I grasped that I, too, was an heir, and began to apply myself as one who expected to succeed.

You, dear hearts, are Abraham's seed; there is nothing you cannot do according to God's promises. We are no longer estranged from God. Our position in Christ has absolutely nothing to do with us; it's a gift of grace and remains eternally secure and unchanging.

Lydia: Bending

Acts 16:12–15, 40

Lydia was a seller of purple. Her name may have derived from the country of her origin; she lived in the city of Thyatira, located in Lydia. She is believed to have been a businesswoman, a person of means. Purple was a valuable commodity and was primarily worn by princes and the rich.

Paul met Lydia on his second missionary journey, and she became his first European convert. Being very resourceful, Lydia was later able to help Paul with the expenses associated with his trial. Their relationship and her value to the early church are seen in his writings, especially his letter to the church in Philippi.

Their first meeting, however, was a chance encounter. Paul's initial reason for coming to Asia Minor was a Macedonian call. He had a vision of a man asking him to come and help. Paul wanted to go in a different direction, but God sent him to women gathered on the riverbank.

When Paul went to the river on the Sabbath, expecting to find a place of prayer, one can imagine that he didn't expect to find women. The custom of that day was that it took ten Jewish men to organize a synagogue.

You do not have to orchestrate divine appointments; that's why they are divine! You don't have to worry or fret about being in the right place at the right time. All of your days are ordained. Simply go about your life, praying up and preparing yourself to always being open to possibilities, and our God will line up everything in the universe on your behalf.

One thing that went precisely the way Paul expected was a prayer meeting being held. He was not disappointed. Lydia and the ladies in her prayer band didn't let a little old thing such as the absence of a synagogue stand in the way of their prayers.

Lydia and her friends were receptive and hospitable for this unexpected encounter. Don't let negative thoughts and feelings stand in the way or cause you to miss a God-moment. Too often, when things do not go as planned or we feel as though we were not a part of the original plan, we can allow the enemy to make us feel less-than and become defensive.

Lydia was fully engaged in her encounter with Paul. We do not know if Paul shared his vision with the women or whether or not he was disappointed to find women instead of men. Nevertheless, he found Lydia, a woman whose heart was fully open to receiving a word from God.

Remember this, no matter what it looks like to the natural eye, you are not the understudy or the stand-in; it was your assignment. Hear me now; if you look closely with a heart to receive what God is doing, you will see that you are exactly what is needed.

Reflection

I have occasionally been asked to speak because someone was unable to fulfill the obligation. Early on, I used to feel a little uneasy, especially if I was replacing someone I felt was more qualified than me. It wasn't until one such engagement occurred and I was about to depart that the organizer of the meeting stopped me and said, "Next year, we want you to come for *Arnetta*, not in place of another." For the next three years, I was invited to return as their keynote speaker. Your gifts will always make room for you and cause people to see who you are and your value to the Kingdom's work.

Galatians 3:27–29 says not only are we included but we are also heirs. As heirs, we have a responsibility to uphold. Our joy should not be rooted in just having a seat at the table. We have a responsibility to be fully present, fully engaged.

God's plan includes us as *agents of change.*

Being an agent of change should be our lifestyle. Wherever we go and whatever we are called to do, it should always be with the mindset to do good. "Now what I am commanding you today is not too difficult for you or beyond your reach" (Deuteronomy 30:11). I truly believe we can command our day to do good. If this is what we expect, this is what we will receive. Oh, it won't eliminate life's problems, but it will give you a choice to make a difference in responding to the problems. If you walk into a situation with the feeling that your presence was unexpected or a disappointment, you can decide your response.

My very first speaking engagement was one such occasion. I was sent to speak for a women's retreat at a popular Church of God campground with the theme of *Together We Reconcile.*

Let me set the stage. The lady who invited me to speak had a family emergency and could not attend at the last minute. The board member who recommended me to this lady was not there because of personal illness. I was very new to my position, and I am unsure if my picture had been circulated. The look of shock when I walked into the room was one that could not be denied.

It was very uncomfortable at that moment and did not improve as the evening progressed. During dinner, as I sat alone eating, one lady approached me and said, "Now who invited you?" I surely did not feel included. To help regain my composure, I reached out to a family member and shared my feelings of rejection; the tears flowed freely.

I had to speak after dinner, and my feelings were hurt; I could not imagine why God would do this. I thought, *How am I going to stand before these women and preach on reconciliation?* I was too new and nervous to improvise, so I plowed on with my notes in hand.

As the weekend passed, God began to tear down the walls of hostility and separation. I led the ladies in an exercise to build a birdhouse, which allowed us to laugh and work together. I am so glad I didn't retreat, run, or sneak out in the middle of the night, which was my first thought.

Once my presentation was over (I spoke three times throughout the weekend), I went to my room to pack while they held their board meeting. As I was about to depart, one of the sisters asked me to join them. They presented me with one of the birdhouses that had been signed by every lady in the room. It is one of my most treasured memories. Today, the signatures and comments are fading because of time, but that God-moment memory is sealed in my heart forever.

Let the Spirit of God work through you in spite of you. God intended for you to be in that place, make a difference, break through barriers, and pull down strongholds that impede unity. Although it had at first appeared to be one of the most horrid times in my ministry to date, I left smiling because it taught me many valuable lessons. One of the best things I learned that day, which has kept me in good stead, is that God will use me for his glory if I am available and all in. The pain of that experience was not in vain because when I reflect on those moments now, I am filled with praise.

God included you; just be yourself. *Be authentic!* Lydia was an affluent woman, but she was also known as a worshiper. There seemed to be no pretense in her. In just a few Scripture passages regarding Lydia's contribution, we see the full person God valued jump off the pages. She was a lover of God, family, and the people of God. She was a life-learner and always open to new revelations. She was a giver; her wealth was not to showcase her net worth but to provide resources for the relief and the expansion of the Kingdom. She was loyal; Paul and Silas knew they could depend on her in tough times.

It's hard to be authentic when you are not comfortable in your own skin. Sometimes our desire for inclusion can lead us to act out of character or to try to be something we are not. I have known and am blessed to be friends with some of the greatest preachers in this movement, who just happen to be women. I am friends with women who are intellectually brilliant by anyone's standards. I enjoy the richness of our conversations and the sisterhood we have established. They are my friends, my accountability partners, my on-call theologians, and my personal strategists when I need to solve a problem. Each one of us brings something of value to the relationship. We don't compete or undermine one another. We don't get a chance to see one another often, but when we do, hours later, there is still laughter in the room.

Be who you are. God calls you and your personality. The loudest voice in the room, God needs you! The quiet-spoken woman sitting in the corner, God needs your unpretentious personality to confound the world. You are fearfully and wonderfully made—be true to who God has called you to be. Surround yourself with folk who will celebrate you, inspire you, and always make room for you at the table.

Live in the moment with confidence and always be open to ways of improving and growing in grace.

Lydia was a part of God's plan not just for her inclusion only but for her family as well. My sister, you may be the beginning of a legacy of salvation in your family. Since God included you, *live accordingly*. Live so others can see Christ in your life, and they too will become Kingdom citizens.

Lydia's story was one of watching the expansion of the Kingdom in her home and her community. Because her heart was open to receive Paul's message, she and her household were saved. They wanted what she had. Her life was contagious.

We have a responsibility to share the good news with everyone, especially our families. In our quest to be included in and on larger platforms, let us not neglect our families. I remember days I had to turn my car around or cancel an engagement because my children needed me. I didn't want their memories of their mom, the traveling preacher, to be all the days she was away. No, I was determined that they would have memories of all the *Jeopardy!* episodes we watched as a family, the prom pictures I captured, the movie nights I orchestrated, and the moments we attended church together. God's plan for my life included my family, as well. Live accordingly with an appropriate response to who you say you are.

God has included you because the work of the Kingdom needs a few more of what folks in Italy might call *affidabile* people—those we can rely on. Lydia was a friend to Paul; she was affidable. She provided a safe place for him and the other leaders.

After Paul and Silas left Lydia's home, they were stripped, beaten, and put into prison. But when they were released, it was Lydia's home where they found solace. It was a place where prayers were surely voiced. Her home became a haven: a place for refreshing. Our inclusion should also bring comfort to those in need.

Conclusion

You were not an afterthought in the mind of God. You were on his mind just the way you are. What he has purposed for you to do is not by happenstance. Paul didn't just happen upon Lydia; his assignment was to spread the gospel to the Gentiles. Lydia was a major part of that expansion—the first, as a matter of record.

When you are tempted to feel undervalued, out of sync, or like an afterthought, dispel those thoughts. You were there because you are part of the fabric in the quilt. The story or event cannot be adequately told without your contribution. Even the unnamed women in this story had a role. Lydia was not alone: "We sat down and began to speak to the women who had gathered there" (Acts 16:13).

Surround yourself with folk who believe in you and make room for others as well. There's enough work in the Kingdom for each of us to have a place.

Questions for Reflection

1. Lydia was described as a worshiper of God. If someone were to describe you, what adjectives or epithets would that person use?
2. In what areas do you struggle to accept and believe in your giftedness?
3. Who or what were those things that demanded you work up to your potential? Who encouraged, pushed, and refused to let you accept ordinary?

CHAPTER 3

God's Plan Is Inclusive of Others

Do nothing out of selfish ambition or vain conceit. Rather, in humility value others above yourselves, not looking to your own interests but each of you to the interests of the others.
—Philippians 2:3–4

Paul loved the people of the church in Philippi; they were his "joy and crown" (Philippians 4:1). This letter is one that can easily be translated for the modern church. It is an important reminder to us amid societal norms that say wealth, possessions, and notoriety are qualities necessary to define success. The theme of this book says, "Not so!" We must see ourselves as partners with Christ, always striving to live as servants, exalting the Lord above all.

No matter how established we may be, it is not by *our* power or *our* might. Look for ways and opportunities to use your gifts to help another sister walk in her calling. When we focus less on ourselves and more on the needs of others, God will be glorified.

Too often, as we near a transitional period, retirement, or the end of a long assignment, we look for validation. We may allow the uncertainty of the unknown to cause us to self-elevate. In our desire to finish strong, we can lose sight of who we are and whose we are. My dear sister, use this season as an opportunity to bring to bear all the years of experience, successes, failures, moments of clarity, and life through paradigm shifts to offer wisdom and guidance to those coming behind you.

A most familiar passage says, "He who began a good work in you will carry it on to completion" (Phillipians 1:6). No matter the age or season, God's plan includes you. You may feel that you are in a season of uncertainty and change; however, know that God will yet complete what he began. It may be a season where God is not only expanding your life and borders, but he is also giving you the opportunity to help expand borders for others.

Deborah: Be Inviting

Judges 4—5

We, as women, hear so many voices—declarations that call us to action, self-fulfillment, self-improvement, higher self-esteem, and any other method to advance or enlighten. Those things are necessary, but they cannot override what is needed most. Women of faith, we are called to stand courageously for truth and righteousness as a standard for living and as a guide for others to follow. Our lives have to be the declaration.

Deborah was one such woman. Yes, she was a woman of action, self-fulfilled, but more importantly, her life spoke truth to power. Deborah's vision was inclusive of others—not inwardly focused but with a strong desire that empowered others. She was willing to invest time and resources to help others succeed, especially another woman.

The stories of the Old Testament reflect a male-oriented society. Within this framework, men inspired by God deemed it necessary to share Deborah's story with great appreciation for her leadership. Deborah was a prophetess and wife of Lappidoth. Her introduction speaks volumes about who she was and the correct succession of titles. We first see her relationship with God as a prophetess, then her relationship with her family as a wife, and finally her ministry as a judge. Too often, because women are so great at multi-tasking, we can lose balance. We can let the ministry supersede our relationship with God or family.

A healthy and effective ministry is spiritually sensitive to obstacles, burnout, and temptations before they overtake it. God is the first and center of everything. When we understand and seek him first, we won't strive so hard to be counted but will find peace in the knowledge that what God has ordained for us will come to pass. The fear of being overshadowed by others will fade, and we can enter into divine appointments with ease and not miss alliances that are beneficial for everyone.

Deborah was a judge during a crisis; her influence was noticeable to a major military leader, Barak. While she lived in southern Ephraim, her influence went as far north as Naphtali and Zebulun. Deborah spoke with godly authority. Israel had once again turned to idolatry, and a new period of oppression had begun that had lasted twenty years. This was the backdrop of Deborah's entry into Israel's history. Jabin was the oppressing king, and Sisera was the captain of his army with many chariots of iron. He was causing terror among the Israelites, who were without equal weaponry.

Deborah, known as the Mother of Israel, held court under the Palm of Deborah. When everyone else was fearful and uncertain, she believed God: "She sent for Barak son of Abinoam from Kedesh in Naphtali and said to him, 'The LORD, the God of Israel, commands you: "Go, take with you ten thousand men of Naphtali and Zebulun and lead them up to Mount Tabor. I will lead Sisera, the commander of Jabin's army, with his chariots and his troops to the Kishon River and give him into your hands" ' " (Judges 4:6–8).

Barak is often given a bad rap because of his dependence on Deborah. However, I see this event differently. Barak had to be keenly aware of Deborah's reputation as a strong, courageous, and trustworthy leader. Those are the people we want with us when we go into battle. Some commentaries have questioned his manhood because of his confidence in this woman. He was confident in Deborah's abilities, strength of character, and reputation as a judge. Barak saw the leader, not a woman. "There is neither…male [nor] female" (Galatians 3:28)—we are all equal in God's sight.

Barak's mistake was not his trust in Deborah's strengths, but his lack of faith in the one who can do anything but fail—the one who declared to Deborah, "I will lead Sisera…and give him into your hands" (Judges 4:7). Barak's faith in Deborah was misplaced; it should not have exceeded his faith in God. His desire for Deborah to accompany him was not a blotch on his manhood, but an acknowledgment of her strength.

Nevertheless, because of this error, Deborah declared, "Certainly I will go with you…. But because of the course you are taking, the honor will not be yours, for the LORD will deliver Sisera into the hands of a woman" (Judges 4:9). When I first heard the telling of this story, my mind had moved ahead before the teacher could finish. Deborah to the rescue; she would be the victor. Girl power! Something inside of me leaped as the teacher completed the story. I sat taller in my seat with a renewed sense of pride in sisterhood. Something rose in me, and I literally cheered. Deborah became a heroine and role model that I wanted to emulate.

Reflection

Too often, women have been viewed as unsupportive of one another and selfishly seeking personal gain at the cost of others. This story is a story of true sisterhood, reflecting an experience that I have known well and celebrate. It is one I follow every chance given. I feel we all win when someone from our tribe is leaving her mark, and we know that in some small way we were a part of that process.

Deborah's vision of defeat at the hand of a woman was not for her, but it was for the generation following. Deborah believed God's plan was for the *advancement* of his people. It was bigger than her or Barak. My sweet sister, we may never be able to fulfill all the things we want to do, but when we speak life and hope over the next generation and invest in them, they will carry our hearts.

I believe every generation has a purpose. Even as I near this transitional season of life, I know that I have lived, seen, and accomplished things my parents never could have imagined. So it is for those who follow us that we should do all we can to help them advance. They will break down barriers that plague us today.

This is 2021, and I truly believe the racial divides that we are currently struggling with will not be those of our children. I am not naïve enough to believe that everything will disappear, but some things will die with our generation. The lens by which my children and grandchildren view life is much different from mine. We raised them in a multi-cultural environment, and they will not carry the same biases. Their world is much more inclusive than ours.

Traveling has been a part of my assignment. Over the last few years, I have found more young women desiring to travel with me and seeking mentoring. More often than not, I have said *yes* to this budding relationship. Why? Because I remember. Once when I asked a more seasoned woman to mentor me, she said *yes*, but as time went on, she would never return my calls. I don't think harshly of her actions; life probably got in the way, and she didn't know how to say *no*—that's another lesson.

However, I remember how that rejection made me feel. I promised myself years later that I would not make the same mistake in judgment. I promised that if I ever said *yes* to investing time in mentoring and guiding another in ministry, I would take that assignment seriously and never let anyone feel my rejection.

My travels with young women are not for them to carry my luggage but to carry my dreams. As the years have progressed, I have found that ministry is a relay; it's not about who carries the baton last as long as God gets the credit for the race. Tim Keller says, "If our identity is in our work, rather than in Christ, success will go to our heads and failure will go to our hearts."[1]

While this book is written with my sisters in mind, it is an equal-opportunity message. Deborah accompanied Barak on his mission and never wavered in her belief that God would give the victory to Israel on the battlefield. There are times when it is necessary to *accompany* others for moral support. Yet, never lose sight of the fact that the help you provide comes from God.

While accompanying Barak, Deborah said, "Go! This is the day the Lord has given Sisera into your hands. Has not the Lord gone ahead of you?" (Judges 4:14). God caused a great storm and a sudden cloudburst, which immobilized the Canaanites. The Israelites took such courage in seeing God causing them to triumph that they aggressively advanced and slew many of the Canaanites.

Sisera, the one who had chafed and terrorized the Israelites, fled as he witnessed the defeat of his army. He escaped to Heber the Kenite's tent; Heber was a descendant of Moses' in-laws and was known to have a friendly relationship with King Jabin. Sisera felt at ease in the safety of this tent, but then Jael, the wife of Heber, entered. It is apparent that her loyalties were not those of her husband; Jael's heart was with Israel.

I am grateful for those who poured into me, who walked with me when I hadn't yet found my strength. Because of them, I carry their dreams of a better church and a better world. They refused to let us die; they snatched many of us out of harm's way and refused to leave us to our own devices. These determined servant-leaders reminded us of God's promises. Ladies, don't miss an opportunity to help someone succeed. Be careful not to allow others' dependence, however, to be placed on you. Guide, assist, and nudge them into the ways of the Lord.

---

1 Tim Keller, Twitter post, April 16, 2015, https://twitter.com/dailykeller.

Jael was daring and probably found it difficult to live with her family's betrayal of Israel. Jael's name meant "wild she-goat"; she was a fighter. She broke their tradition of hospitality. Clearly, her act of loyalty on behalf of the Israelites was part and parcel of God's plan. Jael did not have time to plot or strategize the demise of Sisera; she took advantage of the opportunity.

Ladies, make room for the audaciousness of the next generation. We, too, were like them: bold and sometimes spontaneous. Don't be *afraid* of their ambition. Don't try to harness it but provide guidance. Jael was a tent woman; she used the implements before her, the things she was familiar with: a peg and a hammer.

The methods of our children may be unfamiliar to us or used differently from what we are accustomed to. Don't get distracted or disillusioned by their methods. Methods change, but the message does not. Their love for God is just as real as ours. I remember praying the Prayer of Jabez in the '90s. Our prayers were big for that day that God would bless us indeed.

We asked God for more, and he answered our prayers. Small groups formed, ministries flourished, our confidence and our faith increased. The COVID-19 pandemic has forced many of us to social-media platforms we had previously resisted. We found that many of our children's methods now have merit. Technology is their peg and hammer for today. Their reach is much broader than we could imagine.

Don't be frightened of their boldness and drive; give them the best that you have. One of the best gifts we can give to those following us is our confidence in who they are and what they have to offer. Deborah's gift to Jael was acknowledging her value. God would bring victory through the hands of a woman, and that woman was Jael. Friends, we have the ability to pave the way, lend our voice, and call forth more fearless women of God.

Jael's killing of Sisera is often questioned by theologians and historians and seen as treacherous. Deborah prophesied Sisera's death—maybe not the details, but the outcome. Jael's actions were a clear statement of her position to be on the side of God's chosen people. Her act was in line with God's purpose.

What do you imagine drove this woman to do what she did? We will never know. Was it patriotism, a need for significance, an opportunity to avenge the mistreatment of the Israelites? Whatever it was, she was devoted to what she believed.

We have an opportunity to help those who are following to remain *faithful to God* and to what they believe while waiting for their turn. Jael was not technically an Israelite, but she was the agent God used. She was committed to what she heard and was willing to act on it. Jael believed the stories about the God of her husband's ancestors. Life could not have been easy for this woman to live this contradiction.

This ambiguity was a part of Jael's existence. It is easy at any age to become impatient and discouraged when we want to see change, especially when we feel as though we have no control. Imagine Jael's frustration. *When will I have the opportunity to speak up and share my true feelings? I am on the side of the Israelites, but I am just a "tent woman." Who will hear me; what can I do to make a difference?* Jael could have brought harm to herself and her family if she had moved before it was time. Something inside of this woman had to be crying to be free.

I have a good friend who once said to me, "Arnetta, God is never just doing one thing at a time." At the same time, God used Barak's fear of going into battle without Deborah and Deborah's assurance of victory at the hands of a woman. This led to a providential encounter between Jael and Sisera, which changed the trajectory of all of their lives. Jael, knowingly or not, had to wait on her turn.

Every one of us has our turn to be used in some way by God. The problem can sometimes be waiting. Do we wait but blame others and become exasperated, or do we wait with a spirit of preparation? What lessons have you learned while waiting? Sister, someone is waiting and needs to hear about that journey, your wise counsel.

We all know of countless people who moved before their time and the disaster that followed. There is value in being faithful while waiting. Elisha had left everything he had to follow the prophet Elijah. As Elijah was about to depart, he asked Elisha, "What can I do for you?" (2 Kings 2:9). The younger man asked for a double portion of what Elijah had. Elijah did not scold his charge for his ambition or for desiring more. The wiser man was honest with him: " 'You have asked a difficult thing,' Elijah said, ‘yet if you see me when I am taken from you, it will be yours—otherwise, it will not’ ” (v 10). It was not an impossible request, but it required something from Elisha. He had to remain faithful.

Deborah—prophetess, wife, and judge—was successful even by today’s standards. Yet her success was not measured by what she accomplished alone. Her relationships with others, her inclusiveness of others and their abilities, distinguished her above many. She was comfortable leading from the back while helping others achieve God’s plan for their lives. John 7:18 says, “Whoever speaks on their own does so to gain personal glory, but he who seeks the glory of the one who sent him is a man of truth; there is nothing false about him.”

Conclusion

How does your bio or fact sheet read? What is the most important thing you want people to know about you? Does it detail all your accomplishments or showcase all the ways God has used you to assist others? It is not necessary to display “false humility” by minimizing the education, skills, or expertise you have acquired; instead, remember that those things do not define you.

When the phone stops ringing and the engagements are few and far between, what memories will bring you the greatest joy? Will it be the academic achievements and accomplishments or the precious moments spent with family and friends? Maybe, just maybe, it will be the times you recall taking a back seat so another sister could shine.

Questions for Reflection

1. Whom do you include on your journey? Who has included you?
2. In what areas of your life and ministry have you lost balance? Where are you striving when you should be thriving?
3. Whom do you identify with more: Deborah, whom others looked toward for leadership, or Barak, who often sought others instead of God for direction? How can these situations dishonor or honor God?

PART 2

God's Purpose

CHAPTER 4

God's Purpose Is to Bring Wholeness

Therefore, there is now no condemnation for those who are in Christ Jesus, because through Christ Jesus the law of the Spirit who gives life has set you free from the law of sin and death. For what the law was powerless to do because it was weakened by the flesh, God did by sending his own Son in the likeness of sinful flesh to be a sin offering. And so he condemned sin in the flesh, in order that the righteous requirement of the law might be fully met in us, who do not live according to the flesh but according to the Spirit.
—Romans 8:1–4

Netta, God forgives you, now forgive yourself! For years I lived in the shadow of my sins, hostage to the memories of my life before Christ. I'm not saying I haven't faltered after my decision to follow Christ, but it seems easier to accept God's forgiveness today than those things of yesterday. As a result, I wasted so much time feeling less-than, incomplete, and fractured.

The intercession of Christ, his coming, and his death must put an end to the tension waged within our souls. Your upbringing, your teaching, and your belief system often determine your level of struggle. If we were taught more about what we couldn't do (law) rather than what Christ's coming did, it often restricts our ability to let go. Condemnation from others is a hard road to tread, but it is nothing compared to the condemnation we often place on ourselves.

Paul was encouraging the people to focus on the cross. The law points to sin, but Jesus' coming enables believers to follow after the Spirit. We sometimes find ourselves trusting God's forgiveness for today and yet holding on to the sins of the past. Ladies, God's purpose is that we walk in wholeness from the past, in the present, and to the future. “For as high as the heavens are above the earth, so great is his love for those who fear him; as far as the east is from the west, so far has he removed our transgressions from us” (Psalm 103:11–12). Christ’s intervention in your life erased the hold of your past. Don’t be held hostage to the sins of the past; remember that every experience, no matter how much shame or blame might be associated with it, was not in vain.

The Samaritan Woman: The Woman Who Left Her Old Life Behind

John 4:4–42

Have you had that moment when you really knew you were separated from the past? That moment of clarity when a message, a song, or a scripture touched the deep recesses of your heart, and you knew you were forgiven? Oh, how I pray if that has not happened yet, that while engaging in this chapter, you too will leave your water jar and live in abundance. I pray that this chapter will be a catalyst to discovering your appointed destiny.

From the beginning of time, God's purpose was that we live full lives—not fragmented, incomplete, or lacking but full, productive lives. It is articulated so well through the words of Jesus: "I have come that they may have life, and have it to the full" (John 10:10).

Historically there was an estrangement between Jews and the Samaritans. The hostility can be traced back to the Assyrian colonization. The breach between the Samaritans and the Jews escalated with the formation of the northern kingdom of Israel under the reign of Jeroboam I. The conflicting difference was the true location to worship God. The Samaritans believed it was Mount Gerizim, not Mount Zion. This was followed by the antagonism of the Samaritans to the Jews at the return of captivity, recorded in the books of Ezra and Nehemiah. This breach mattered none to Jesus.

Prejudice has always been prevalent in the history of humankind. The Jews and the Samaritans were more alike than different. However, they could only see the differences. Each group sought a good life and family security; each had hopes, dreams, and desires. They suffered from the same maladies of life, yet a racial hatred kept them apart.

Even as I write this chapter, our world, especially this nation, is fragmented. We are divided by race, religion, gender, class, and political preference, just to name a few. We, as a nation, were founded under the banner of "One Nation under God." It is clear that times were not perfect even when this was adopted, but it was at least the guiding principle that drew people together. Today, however, the hostility between our population's segments as mentioned above has left us in pieces: unwilling to talk, listen, or seek to understand our differences.

Jesus chose an unpopular road for a Jew to travel. He was on his way to Galilee from Judea and stopped at Jacob's well to rest. He was deliberate on this day, as he always is when it comes to you and me. Jesus modeled for us in this story the way to live above religious and racial prejudices.

This unnamed woman met Jesus at a well near Sychar. Just by the very nature of the cultural differences, Jesus' reaction to her presence could have been one of condemnation. It would have been understandable because Samaritans were seen as outcasts: despised, avoided, and looked upon as less-than by the Jews. Being a woman during this period of time had its own challenges. Women had no power; they were subject to their fathers and then their husbands. Only the husband could petition for divorce.

Yet, this is the person whom Jesus had to see, had to have a conversation with. Why? Because, despite what was known, felt, and seen by others, God had a purpose, a good purpose for her life. Jesus was willing to go against all the social norms of the day to alleviate this woman's suffering and shame and make her whole again. Her encounter that day not only changed the trajectory of her life but also those of her family and her community.

Why would she go at noon, the hottest time of the day? Many have speculated it was to avoid the people's glances, the gossipy ladies, maybe the men's taunts. My sister, we no longer have to run from the shadows of our past. We no longer have to duck and dodge those who point fingers and remember. The Word tells us we overcome "by the blood of the Lamb and by the word of [our] testimony" (Revelation 12:11). Do not allow anyone to hold you hostage to your past; use your story for good and for God's glory.

What Jesus accomplished with this Samaritan woman was open dialogue. If you notice in the story, he isolated them so that a productive conversation could take place. If the disciples had been present, the outcome might have been entirely different. Why do I say this? Because as soon as they returned, they "were surprised to find him talking with a woman" (John 4:27).

May I encourage you, dear heart, to look for opportunities to have open dialogue, real talk. It may be that you must step away from your group, your peers, your familiar tribe so you can hear and receive a word that will help bring a broader perspective of life into view for you.

Jesus' one-on-one conversation with this woman at Jacob's well was about to be transformational. She knew the Pentateuchal law against adultery, but now she was about to learn a more valuable lesson, the love of Christ. She would find out in this brief encounter that nothing done in her past, present, or future would "separate [her] from the love of God that is in Christ Jesus our Lord" (Romans 8:39).

Many of us can identify personally with this unnamed woman. Maybe you have not been in multiple relationships as this woman had, but there are certainly things in your life that have caused you to hide out, avoid people, or live in shame.

We live our lives just a moment removed from our past. What we have done is always on repeat in our thoughts and hearts. We live so concerned by and focused on others' opinions of us that we don't live in our fullness because we deplete ourselves daily of the future's wonderful possibilities.

This woman's first thought was, "How can you ask me for a drink?" (v 9). Filled with emotions, traditions, and thoughts that detach and disconnect, how often have we labeled others or even ourselves at first glance before a word was even spoken? God's purpose for his creation is that we live in community, not alone.

Jesus said, "If you knew" (v 10)! If we knew that he came so we might have life. If we knew that God so loved us. If we knew that he does not want anyone to perish. If we knew that he is faithful and just and will forgive us our sins and purify us from all unrighteousness. If we only knew the plans God had for our lives, we would respond so differently to life's circumstances.

Jesus offered this woman the gift of God. This gift has the power to override the unquenchable thirst of trying to do it on our own. Without opening our hearts to receive this gift, we will continue to repeat the same things over and over and never find satisfaction.

Jesus said, "Whoever drinks the water I give them will never thirst" (v 14). Jesus was offering sustenance for living. It was not a one-time occurrence, not just a drip but a fountain springing up from within. The Samaritan woman had a glimpse of what life could be and desired what Jesus had to offer: "Sir, give me this water so that I won't get thirsty and have to keep coming *here* to draw water" (v 15, emphasis added).

Where, what, or who is your *here*? *Here* stands between you and God; it steals your joy; it's an illusion of happiness. Unfortunately, it does not last. It only brings momentary satisfaction, and it keeps you trying to rekindle that fleeting moment of pleasure.

All of us have experienced a *here* at one time or another. It may have begun as a good experience, and then it turned toxic. If it distracts or destroys your intimate relationship with God, it must go. Jesus' question forced the woman to identify her *here*. It was relationship issues, clearly, because she had five husbands and was now with a man who was not her husband.

There is nothing you can say to God that surprises him. Your past choices will not catch him off guard or leave him speechless. Before she could even confess, Jesus' response was, in essence, "I know, and thank you for being honest."

Often the journey to living full lives is our ability to be honest with both God and ourselves. We may be able to hide and avoid the gaze of others, but God sees and knows. Don't try to deflect what the problem is. Own up to your choices and then you can move on.

I have encountered so many people who are stuck in pain and shame because they try to reason or rationalize their behavior. "If he had, if that didn't...then I would have made a different choice." No matter what others do, it is always our responsibility to do the right thing. It is always on us to make better choices and try to live so that we have no regrets. This may not be easy, but it is certainly worth a try.

Jesus said to the woman, "A time is coming when you will worship the Father neither on this mountain nor in Jerusalem" (v 21). In other words, all these reasons we have to disagree will not matter in the end. What is important is our worship.

Worship is not what we do in our churches on Sunday morning. COVID-19 has taught us that. Worship is the act of exalting God to a place of honor and reverence because he is worthy. Worship is how we live; it is a lifestyle. Worship is honoring God. It is sacrificial. It is how we love God and each other. It is how we serve.

The story ends with the Samaritan woman leaving her water jug behind and telling everyone she encountered, "Come, see a man who told me everything I ever did. Could this be the Messiah?" (v 29).

This story has had two major effects on my life. It has taught me to forgive myself and reconcile (settle) forever that God has a purpose for my life. I once preached a message very early on in ministry entitled, "Even Me." The sad part of this truth is that I still didn't believe it in my heart while preaching this message.

But today, I walk boldly in the light of the Samaritan woman's memory, "Come, see a man who told me everything I ever did," with my addition to the text, "and it did not matter!"

Reflection

The Samaritan Woman had been living in the shadow of her sin, hiding out and trying to go unnoticed. What a sad commentary when we allow the enemy to convince us that our situation is hopeless or helpless. If that is you today, dispel that notion immediately before you move to the next sentence. There is nothing you have done that cannot be washed away by the blood of Jesus. Your sin is not greater than the grace of God. God's love will dissolve the sting of your past to make way for his purpose for your future.

We miss so much because we continue to carry that "water jar" which represents past sins, things of shame, places of blame, insecurities, denial, dysfunction, family hurts, relationship failures—you fill in the blank. What are you still holding on to because you think your circumstance is unique to God? Why can you not fully accept forgiveness? One day you walk in wholeness, but you feel as though you are at the beginning of your faith the next day. The enemy of your mind and thoughts has convinced you that your faults or choices were so egregious that even God's grace is not enough. Oh, but it is.

Often we hold on to the *if only you knew* guilt, as though what we have experienced or done is too big for even God to handle, but it is not. Jesus saw into the depths of this woman's life, and it did not matter what she had done. Christ knows it all, and there is nothing we can do that has or will separate us from his love. Oh, how I wish these words were not just cliché for us, but an infallible promise that we would depend on daily.

For all of my twenties and most of my thirties, I was addicted to drugs. I do not say that with pride, but I am proud of my testimony. Every time the enemy has tried to hold me hostage, I am reminded of Revelation 12:10–11, which says:

> Then I heard a loud voice in heaven say:
> "Now have come the salvation and the power
> and the kingdom of our God,
> and the authority of his Messiah.
> For the accuser of our brothers and sisters,
> who accuses them before our God day and night,
> has been hurled down.
> They triumphed over him
> by the blood of the Lamb
> and by the word of their testimony."

Let me provide the *Reader's Digest* version of my conversion. It was a cataclysmic moment in my life. I was sitting at a table with plans of spending the entire evening indulging in this habit. The voice of God spoke very clearly in my head, "Arnetta, what are you doing here?" I ignored the first two times, questioning my friend if she indeed was talking to me. When she replied with frustration the second time, I knew it was God speaking. I removed myself from that setting and have never had a desire to go back.

Two years later, after giving my heart to God, my pastor, Dr. Eustace Rawlings, asked me to teach a lesson on a Wednesday night. Unbeknownst to him, he gave me the subject of drug addiction. I avoided that assignment for three months. I knew that my story would be shocking and disappointing to many. Yes, I was frightened that they would look at me differently. Even as I write this experience, I have a certain level of discomfort regarding the response of the reader. But, how many of you believe as I do? God's *yes* is louder than your *no*! I do not share this story for impact but to encourage those struggling with an addiction, stronghold, or emotional instability that has robbed them of being who God created them to be. Stop now, and ask God to help you; he will!

After God "outed" me, he began to speak into my spirit, "There will be healing in your testimony." And I found that to be true! A few years later, he birthed Priscilla's Lost and Found and In the Company of Good Men through me. These mentoring programs were designed to reach the lost. For sixteen years and eight chapters throughout the United States, we were blessed to touch thousands of lives with the gospel. One of the fundamental reasons for the birth of Priscilla's Lost and Found was my testimony. While many of my choices were certainly regrettable, my journey was not in vain.

God used my past to inform my future. My service in the local congregation and ministry to the community strengthened my skills in administration and outreach. When offered the opportunity to work in national ministries, I resisted for months. I could not see how my passion for ministry to the margins would align itself with what I knew of the position with Women of the Church of God. My perception was that it focused heavily on overseas missions and very little on the mission fields at home, in our neighborhoods and communities.

As I began leadership of Women of the Church of God, a ministry born out of the need to support missionaries, I wondered how effective I could be. Overseas missions had never been a strong part of my congregational ministry. While we certainly supported the work of missions, missionaries did not usually visit African American congregations. Our information was gathered through brochures and a once-a-year candlelight service during the Wednesday-night Anderson Camp Meeting.

As much as I tried to hide, blend in, and go unnoticed, God brought this burden to the forefront. While I verbally shared my testimony less and less as the years progressed, I tried to live it every day. Yet anyone who knows me well knows my passion for lost souls. There is nothing that excites me more than witnessing a life being transformed by the Spirit of God.

During my tenure as executive director of the ministry, I never lost my desire, but God expanded my global view. He allowed me to think *missional* as a way of life. I was blessed to have a board that heard my heart and followed what we believed was the leading of the Lord. We made a concerted effort to no longer be just supporters of missions and missionaries but to see ourselves as missionaries as well. Every one of us has an opportunity to tell someone.

The story of the Samaritan woman leaves us to imagine that this woman spent much of her life looking for love, acceptance, validation, or intimacy. Who knows what it was, but clearly she had not found it until she met Jesus. How many years do we waste and how much energy do we exert trying to find out who we are? Mark Twain is reported to have said, "The two most important days in your life are the day you are born and the day you find out why." For so many people, the latter is connected to our new birth in Christ. We were created to glorify God through our lives. We were made by God for God, and it is for his pleasure that we exist and were created.

Our purpose for being is never overshadowed in seasons of darkness. The Samaritan woman *discovered* she had a voice that overrode her vices, her defects, and her faults. I love the lyrics of the song "He Looked Beyond My Fault and Saw My Need." When the story of the Samaritan woman began, we saw a woman living in the shadows; her exchange with Jesus was void of joy or hope for a future. One could imagine that she had resolved that she would always be where she was.

I pray your study of this woman outside the pages of this book will enable you to see the veil; it's never too late. I was forty years old when my life finally came into view. I had been married for fifteen years and was blessed with wonderful children, yet I did not have a clue of who I was. I was living everyone else's definition of my existence.

If you are over the age of fifty, at least once in your life you have probably heard the phrase "Sticks and stones may break my bones…." This idiom is often used to help children cope with verbal bullying. Do not allow the criticism, taunts, or untruths to sway you, hurt you, or distract you from moving forward.

Sister, we must live above harmful words or undeserved criticism in the name of helping us grow. We are so much more than unfavorable social media posts, physical appearance, skin color, labels, career choice, titles, betrayal of friends, material possessions, income, or lack thereof. There is no attack, blame, disapproval, judgment, or criticism that matters more than what God says. We are more than conquerors over a situation—past, present, or future.

The older I have gotten, the more I realize that the voice we must overcome the most is the one inside our heads. How many times have we allowed our thinking to stand in the way of doing something we really wanted to do but avoided because we felt inferior? We avoided people and failed to say *yes* when asked to serve because we had not fully accepted that we are new creations. That is equivalent to going to our own private wells at noon. We wear an invisible shroud of shame, which has left us unfulfilled and thirsty.

I was introduced to a book that is now out of print called *The Misconception about Purpose* by David E. Martin. I delved into the study of the Word with fervor, using this book as a devotional, and it led me on a journey of discovery.

Ladies, we will never know who we are or what God's will is for our lives unless we know his Word! Plain and simple. Jesus said to the woman, "A time is coming and has now come when the true worshipers will worship the Father in the Spirit and in truth, for they are the kind of worshipers the Father seeks. God is spirit, and his worshipers must worship in the Spirit and in truth" (John 4:23–24). Our truth is in our relationship with God. Jesus was taking the woman from the superficial to the spiritual. Her discovery that she was talking with Jesus empowered her to live.

What this woman had been searching for was now satisfied in Jesus alone. Before the apostle Peter penned these words, this woman lived them: "But you are a chosen people, a royal priesthood, a holy nation, God's special possession, that you may declare the praises of him who called you out of darkness into his wonderful light" (1 Peter 2:9).

Those whom others speak of with contempt, condemnation, and disgust are just the kind of people Jesus had dealings with. They are the ones God uses to make the greatest impact. Think of his disciples, Mary Magdalene, or the woman with the alabaster jar. Jesus modeled for us that he was above racial and social prejudices. He was no respecter of persons. He came to seek and save the lost and that, dear hearts, includes all of us.

After her encounter with Jesus, the Samaritan woman lived freely. There was no mention in later passages of her sin, only her salvation and its impact on her community. She lived beyond the labels. We are not our mistakes; we are miracles. We are not our abuse; we are amazing.

This woman, who represents you and me, now lived as one of the children of the light. She *deployed* herself. She went into action for a deliberate purpose, to spread the good news. Jesus sparked something on the inside of this woman that was beyond her capacity to contain, and she became the first woman evangelist. What he gave her was for eternity.

My sister, it's deployment time. There is healing in your testimony. Stop allowing what happened in the past to limit what God has in store for you in the future. Who knows, the place of your pain may be the very place God would have you return to bring healing.

We have been sidetracked by shame, given in to fear and doubt, and been discouraged by what others have said to us. Someone is waiting for your testimony. In *The Misconception about Purpose*, it says, "There are thousands of songs never written, messages never preached, thousands of sick never visited, churches never established. There are thousands of books never written, prisoners never visited, children never taught about Jesus" because we failed to allow God to fulfill his purpose in our lives.[2]

The Samaritan woman left her old way of thinking—thinking that had crippled her movements. And she believed God for the living water, welling up to eternal life.

Conclusion

Author Sheila Walsh says, "Perhaps the greatest piece in your witnessing wardrobe is your own story of what Christ has done for you. You never know when you'll need to pull it out."[3]

Questions for Reflection

1. Are you living in the shadow of who God purposed you to be? How has this chapter spoken to you and brought clarity?

2. How will you live above harmful words from this day forward?

3. What new opportunities has God brought into your life?

2 David E. Martin, *The Misconception about Purpose* (n.p.: privately printed), 11.
3 Sheila Walsh in *Women of Character: Ninety Days of Inspirational Readings to Affirm, Strengthen and Encourage the Woman of Character*, ed. Lawrence Kimbrough (Nashville: B & H Publishing Group, 1998), 152.

CHAPTER 5

God's Purpose Is for Us to Bring Forth

"Ye have not chosen me, but I have chosen you, and ordained you, that ye should go and bring forth fruit, and that your fruit should remain."
—John 15:16a, KJV

The union between Jesus and us is not an external agreement; it is personal. He gives us meaning and substance. His love for us says, "*You did not choose me, but I chose you.*" Jesus validates his children and sends us out into the world to continue his mission.

The search for validation began in the garden of Eden with Cain and Abel. If Cain had believed his sacrifice was acceptable, there would be no need for him to despise his brother's gift. We do not have to earn validation from God; it is ours to claim.

We have been ordained, set apart for a work. I once heard a pastor say God is an "equal opportunity employer." The Lord's words to Jeremiah have no gender distinction: "Before I formed you in the womb I knew you, before you were born I set you apart" (Jeremiah 1:5). Ladies, it is not too late to be who God intended for you to be. Procrastination, fear, and uncertainty are strongholds to keep you bound. It is time to live your *Yes Life*! Say *yes* to whom God has appointed you to be.

You and I were created to bring forth, to bear, to give out. This message is reinforced in the Great Commission: go make disciples. Jesus' words were not optional for believers or selective. Each of us has been chosen to bring forth.

Years ago, we used to sing a song about how only what we do for Christ will be counted in the end. I understand the concept, but I beg to differ. Everything we do will be counted in the end: good or bad. However, what is significant is what we do for Christ: the good we do, the love we freely give, the lives added to the Kingdom because we believed that we were chosen to bring forth fruit that will last.

Mary, Mother of Jesus: Blessed Is She Who Believed

Luke 1:26–55

Blind faith is believing when there is no evidence to support the outcome. Often this advice is given when individuals are faced with situations beyond their control. Usually, it pertains to a crisis, challenge, desire, or need. However, there are times when it seems as though something extraordinary is about to happen in your life, and you feel undeserving. Too often, we run to doubt and fear as a way of protecting our emotions rather than holding fast to our faith and choosing to believe even when we cannot see. I hope that after we unpack the life of Mary, this woman of little means, the next time you are faced with an outcome out of your control, your first reaction will be, *Lord, I believe.*

There are so many facets to Mary's story. We can glean many life lessons from the pronouncement of her pregnancy, Jesus' birth, incidents of his childhood, and, finally, the saddest moment in a parent's life: losing a child. While all of these events could be explored, in this chapter I will dwell only on Gabriel and Mary's encounter and her response to this life-changing news. As I delved more deeply into the life of this woman, I became more excited when I was reminded that the first mention of Mary was found in Genesis 3:15, identifying that the destroyer of Satan would be the offspring of "the woman."

Mary's story can be found in all the Gospels. However, Luke's detailed account of her life also includes the historical scene prior to Mary's entry into the sacred text. Luke provides a more complete version of who she was and her thought process. "In those days Caesar Augustus issued a decree that a census should be taken of the entire Roman world" (Luke 2:1).

What do we know of Nazareth? This was a small, secluded village located in the hills of lower Galilee. This location seemed so insignificant that it was not mentioned in the Old Testament, in the Talmud, or by the historian Josephus. That is until one of its youngest citizens would cause this village to become a widely recognized location, still spoken of with honor over two thousand years later. God often chooses quite unexpected, remote places under unusual circumstances to bring forth special missions. If we accept in faith and obedience, the God of the impossible will always do the possible.

"Nathanael said to him, 'Can anything good come out of Nazareth?' " (John 1:46, NKJV). Oh my sister, how does one stay encouraged when there are labels we must overcome before we know we are even in the game? What is our defense to the stereotypes and perceptions others use to undermine, delay, discourage, or even hinder God's purpose for our lives? Our greatest defense is to believe. Mary of Nazareth, a descendant of Nathan, David's son, was chosen by God to be the mother of Jesus. This young virgin from Nazareth stood before the angel Gabriel, sent by God. His message to her would override every notion that she was anything other than special. God sent a messenger from heaven just for her. Why? Because she was chosen. "Greetings, you are highly favored! The Lord is with you" (Luke 1:28). The answer is simple: we must believe! A quick word before you lay this book down in disgust: I know the answer is simple, but the process may prove otherwise. Stay with me.

Mary's response was normal; she was troubled. She was unsettled by the message and the messenger. One of the things I note in her exchange with Gabriel is the question of how she could bear a child since she was a virgin. But she never questioned that she was highly favored or had found favor with God. You may face many things in life that seem like impossibilities, but never question your standing with God.

People may speak against you, where you come from, whether you are qualified or have the right connections, but they can never change God's love for you. "For God so loved the world..." (John 3:16). The opinion of others will never change God's purpose for your life. We could allow their words to stand in our way, but instead let us remember that we are not just conquerors; we are more than conquerors.

Gabriel gave details of what was about to happen to Mary. She would give birth to a son and name him Jesus. This child would not be an average child; he would be great and called the Son of God! Gabriel's prophecy went on to describe Jesus' kingdom and his reign. How blessed we are two thousand years later to celebrate, recognize, and rejoice in the Savior's birth.

When God plants a seed, a thought, or a vision on the inside of us, it is always connected to him. Whatever he brings forth will be great. This greatness may be measured by some according to numbers and popularity, but that is not God's way. If what God has purposed for you to do brings transformation to one life, it has importance.

Have we stopped expecting remarkable things to happen for us? Is it because we are too often living in self-renunciation and self-forgetfulness? If these were tendencies Mary possessed, she took advantage of the moment. The moment is when you realize you are remarkable, and God is with you.

Too often, we keep reaching and searching for significance that can only be found in God. Remember, it is in him that we live. As you reread this story, notice that before Gabriel began to prophesy, he called Mary highly favored and told her that God was with her. These words were not uniquely spoken over Mary; this message that God is with us has been recorded throughout the Scriptures. Paul reminded us of this in Ephesians 1:6. The words he used, "freely given us," have the same meaning in Greek as "highly favored." Each one of us has been made acceptable and given special honor.

Once Gabriel had completed his prophecy to Mary, her response was, "Let it be to me" (Luke 1:38, ESV). My sister, stay in faith. Be resilient and unmovable despite obstacles that come your way. Surely Mary understood what challenges she was about to face. Those challenges included the man she was engaged to, her family, his family, and the community in which she lived. It may have been easier to say, "Lord, can you choose someone else?" All of us, at one time or another, have been given assignments we would rather not have. But God chose us, and the victory is found in our obedience.

Mary's response was not in her own strength or power. Gabriel told her, "The Lord is with you" (Luke 1:28). She understood that no matter what would come her way, she was not alone. "Let it be to me, Lord"—can you allow this phrase to pour out of your soul during moments of uncertainty? "Let it be to me, Lord," when life is transitioning and you are not sure of the direction. "Let it be to me," when God speaks, and it seems impossible. Lean into your faith; God is with you.

God has the power to deliver astonishing things in surprising ways. He delights in giving good gifts to us. Let's keep our hearts and minds open to receive them. Mary was not the only one with astonishing news. Her relative Elizabeth was also pregnant. God will always link you up with the right people who will share in your joy. Mary left and went to stay with Elizabeth for three months. Scripture says that when she arrived, the baby inside of Elizabeth leaped within her womb.

Reflection

I am from East St. Louis, Illinois—not Missouri. I love my hometown. If you Google this place, the first stories to surface are ones of a crime-ridden community, political corruption, poverty, and the per capita murder rate. There is nothing in any of the top stories that speaks of hope or optimism. Nathanael's question regarding Nazareth could easily apply to my hometown. My description would include many of those adjectives. Still, it would also describe resilient people: loyal and committed citizens who refuse to give up or give in. It would include parents, teachers, and neighbors who invested time and resources to create an opportunity for their children's future.

I cannot count the number of times when I have told others where I was from, and the responses were so similar. I get questions about what it's like to live there (as though it were another planet), how I made it out, or how I somehow am the exception to the rule. I assure you that I am not an exception. This city is comprised of so many gifted, resourceful, intelligent people who unfortunately may have missed their opportunity.

I was late coming into who God created me to be. I allowed others' words and perceptions to influence my choices because I was not strong enough to walk in my truth. I have often been underestimated and dismissed before I applied. My hometown was not the only factor in my dismissal; it also was the color of my skin. Before you reject this notion as being too sensitive, it was not. I was kindly told to go away because I was Black. Even today, I realize there is so much more God has in store, according to my faith.

I share this story only to help you believe in who you are and to always remember your value. The origin of your birth, the color of your skin, education, and popularity are not disqualifiers. God will often use what others deem negatives as the very reason to put you in position. I am privileged to have served with amazing men and women who saw me and not society's definition of who they thought I was.

I had served as ministry coordinator with Women of the Church of God (WCG) for five years when I was asked to serve as interim for the three-month sabbatical for the current executive director. I completed that assignment and returned to my role as ministry coordinator. A few months later, the executive director position became vacant, and a search committee was formed. Yes, I certainly thought about applying; however, my lack of faith and confidence stood in the way.

Two events were significant to this story, each one a declaration. Here was my test. Which one would I believe? The first declaration was an encounter with some of the leadership of WCG. Please note, I said some, not all. "Arnetta, we know you can do the job, but the church is not ready for a Black person to serve in this position." I was not surprised by the thought, but I was caught off guard by the messenger. The second declaration was a few weeks later as I lounged at home feeling dejected and uncertain about what to do. My teenage son sat next to me and asked what was wrong. I shared with him my struggle of wanting to apply but not wanting to live out a public rejection if the ministry said *no*. This child looked at me and simply said, "Mom, they rejected Jesus!" Okay, well, alright. The next day I submitted my résumé.

I do not share this story to charge anyone with an offense or to open old wounds. I am retiring soon after serving for fourteen years as executive director. I tell this story to remind you that there will be many declarations in your life. Listen to the one sent from heaven. You will know the difference. "In him we were also chosen, having been predestined according to the plan of him who works out everything in conformity with the purpose of his will" (Ephesians 1:11).

Mary's purpose was to bring forth. God had chosen her for this assignment. It was now up to Mary and her response to the declaration from Gabriel. When Mary *surrendered*, God's purpose was fulfilled in her life. Many of us are on the verge of greatness, but we have not surrendered our will to his will.

Surrendering is not easy! I am the first to admit how difficult it is to let go. I am a planner; I give great attention to detail. I don't want to leave anything to chance. I have to turn off my brain when I am in the middle of a project or an event; all of this would be okay if this trait were restricted to events and projects only. I find myself too often desiring to help God fix it or make it happen.

When Mary surrendered, God was already working on her behalf. God was preparing Joseph's heart to accept Mary's pregnancy. Read Matthew 1:18–24. Mary didn't have to make things right with Joseph; God was at work. Joseph took Mary home as his wife, which protected her in the community. If we are honest, it has not always been easy to come to the place of "not my will, but yours be done" (Luke 22:42). However, life will teach you that it is far better to have a sense of resolve early on that God knows what is best.

Surrender can be uncomfortable, especially for women who have been deemed multi-taskers and doers, who make it happen. How does one move from constant motion to being still—still enough to know and recognize the voice of God during all the noise of life? How does one yield, submit, and relinquish control when society and technology provide all the tools necessary to make things happen quickly?

Today, I give you permission to stop. Listen for the voice of God; let it overrule the to-do list in your head. A surrendered life is a choice. It's the choice to stop striving and start abiding. Stop striving to be the best, to get the promotion, to outsell your neighbor. Matthew 6:33 says, "Seek first his kingdom and his righteousness, and all these things will be given to you as well." If you stop and choose him first, you will be the best, promotions will come, and he will meet all your needs.

This may sound redundant or unnecessary, but I have found it to be true. My first step to surrendering was my confession that I don't want to give up control. It seems that once I confessed what God already knew, the things I needed to acquiesce to became more apparent.

Mary listened to what the angel said regarding her, but she also listened to what he had to say about Elizabeth. It was not a subliminal message; God does not speak to us in codes. He makes his will known. "Even Elizabeth your relative is going to have a child in her old age, and she who was said to be unable to conceive is in her sixth month. For no word from God will ever fail" (Luke 1:36–37). God will connect us with like-minded people.

Surround yourself with folks who will provide support and strength. Mary went to the hill country, to a place of safety. Can you imagine the talk, the gossip, the mean things said to Mary? Elizabeth provided a listening ear and an understanding heart. We all need a friend to run to for a haven: one who is loyal, looking for nothing in return but looking out for our well-being.

Elizabeth celebrated the gift that was coming forth. Surround yourself with people who offer genuine fellowship—those who rejoice at the good news and are not there to stroke your ego. Elizabeth was not worshiping Mary. She said to her, "Blessed are you *among* women" (Luke 1:42, emphasis added), not *above* women. God's purpose to use Mary to bring the Savior into the world did not put her on a pedestal. When people celebrate with you, they are happy for you; when they stroke your ego, they usually want something from you.

Surround yourself with people who will encourage growth and hold you accountable. Elizabeth's greeting to Mary was also a challenge, a reminder of her role and her faith. Every one of us needs an Elizabeth (or a Naomi) in our life, someone who is more mature in some areas, not necessarily in age, but in experience. Such people can see the pitfalls facing you, some of your own making and others that are made by life. However, they are always there to remind you of who you are and your purpose for being.

Surround yourself with friends who seek a sacred life and not the spotlight. Too often, we look for celebration from the masses rather than confirmation from those whom God has set in place to speak into our lives. This is truly the era of living our lives out loud. Everything is on social media. Facebook, Twitter, and Instagram are chronicles for our fifteen minutes of fame. Seek a strong prayer life more than a public status.

When Mary showed up to Elizabeth's house, the baby she was carrying (John the Baptist, forerunner to Christ) leaped in her womb. Throughout the Scriptures, God called his chosen in secret for public assignments.

As we seek to be in relationships according to God's plan for our life, it often means eliminating people as well. I remember when I had to make this decision; it's heart-breaking even today. I loved this woman then, and I love her now, but our close relationship had to end. We had been prayer partners for years and were there for each other in ways stronger than with my blood-sisters. After much prayer, I realized this fact: she would always be a special person in my life, she only needs to call, and I will be there; however, the journey I was now on, she was not a part of. Everyone cannot go with you! Life teaches us that some relationships are for a reason and a season. My wonderful memories of this relationship are not in vain.

Genesis 3:16 pronounced early on that it would not be easy. There would be pain involved. Understanding this from the outset does not change or diminish the results.

"Mary stayed with Elizabeth for about three months and then returned home" (Luke 1:56). It was time to go home. My sister, you *will* survive! Mary understood it was not by her power or might; God was with her. Get up; you will make it.

Mary determined in her heart that, no matter what she had to go through, she would survive. It is hard for me not to begin to preach. This virgin girl believed everything she was told, which equated to everything she needed. "The Holy Spirit will come on you, and the power of the Most High will overshadow you" (Luke 1:35).

God's Spirit, at work in our lives, will take the faith of a mustard seed and move the mountains before us. The enemy would love for us to believe that because we face opposition or competition, we are lacking. Maybe it is because we are tired, weary, worn out, depressed, and under pressure that we don't have the will to fight anymore. Thankfully, the battle is not ours to win.

What God has ordained you to bring forth is the work of the Holy Spirit. You are the vessel God wants to use, but the power is not yours to give. My sister, you have been operating in the shadows too long, unsure and afraid of what God has already spoken over your life. Come forth to bring forth. Ladies, we were created, fashioned, designed to produce or give rise to something great. When we answer the call to bring forth, it will cross all boundaries, barriers, and generation gaps and lift womanhood.

I certainly did not birth Christian Women Connection; that distinction is given to Rev. Nora S. Hunter. She dreamed of broader fields and believed God could use the women within the Church of God to help advance the Kingdom around the world. Nora's vision was born during the depression. It has faced many obstacles time after time. However, since 1932 this ministry continues to aid at home and abroad in the spreading of the gospel.

I did have the honor of birthing Priscilla's Lost and Found as recorded in the previous chapter. For sixteen years, we were blessed to touch lives across this nation and abroad.

Take your place now; step into God's plan and purpose for your life. Folks may have discounted, dismissed, or made fun of what you and what they perceive as impossible. Mary and Elizabeth are true examples of our God, the one who holds all possibility in his hand. You will survive the naysayers and the distractors because "Greater is he that is in you…" (1 John 4:4, KJV).

Conclusion

My friend, colleague, and mentor, the late Dr. Diana Lynn Swoope, authored *Chosen and Highly Favored.* I close with this excerpt from her book: "This means you, my sister. You are no second-class citizen. No longer are you forgotten at the bottom of the pile. No longer are you to see yourself as a victim or an enabler. No longer are you to submerge your intelligence beneath misunderstandings of doctrine and submission. No longer are you to hide your gift, your God-given personality, or your feminine sensitivity. No longer must you accept disrespect simply because you are a woman. God sees you and is speaking to you as the angel spoke to Mary, *Greetings to you, my sister. You are blessed and highly favored.*"[4]

Questions for Reflection

1. Is your lack of faith standing in the way of your next assignment? Explain.
2. How will you let God overrule the "to-do list" in your life and just rest in being?
3. There are people in your life for a season and for a reason. How can you tell the difference?

4 Diana L. Swoope, *Chosen and Highly Favored: A Woman Called to Holiness* (Kansas City: Beacon Hill Press, 2001), 11.

CHAPTER 6

God's Purpose Is to Bring Awareness

There is now no condemnation for those who are in Christ Jesus.... Who will bring any charge against those whom God has chosen? It is God who justifies. —Romans 8:1, 33

There is so much brokenness in this world. For some, there remains a constant struggle to cope, to feel adequate, capable, seen, or even loved. Sin, introduced in the garden of Eden, breached Adam and Eve's relationship with God. It also damaged something on the inside. We live as though we are always afraid of being naked and exposed, so we are always looking for protection and acceptance.

Paul was connecting Romans 8 with the content of the previous chapter. We are powerless over sin; we are weak in our own strength. Therefore, Christ's coming and his involvement should terminate the constant struggle within. Are we good enough? Can we ever overcome our past?

There is no condemnation for those who are in Christ Jesus. There is no attack, blame, disapproval, judgment, or criticism that matters, whether from within or from others. Imagine if Paul had listened to the naysayers who tried to condemn him. Because of his encounter with Jesus, his response was, "The gospel I preached is not of human origin.... I received it by revelation from Jesus Christ" (Galatians 1:11–12).

My sister, God is pleased with you! What if Rahab had never moved past being a harlot? What would have been the future for her family? What if the woman caught in adultery allowed the crowd who wanted to condemn her to be the last voice she received? Yet, she believed Jesus when he said, "Neither do I condemn you.... Go now and leave your life of sin" (John 8:11). She went away free of sin, free to live a complete life.

I had a life before Christ, and it was not pretty. My choices did not say, "One day you will serve in national ministries." I was not on the road to higher living; I was vulnerable to the memories of those who shared some of those experiences with me. Early on, when they found out I was preaching, you could see raised eyebrows and questioning looks. I, too, thought, "How will I ever overcome my past?" I found out that was not my role. My responsibility was to choose Christ; he would do the rest. He has redeemed, vindicated, and restored all that was lost.

Dear friends, walk in the boldness of your faith, "being confident...that he who began a good work in you will carry it on to completion until the day of Christ Jesus" (Philippians 1:6).

The Woman Saved by Grace: Grace in Progress

John 8:1–11

There are so many interesting aspects of this story. Even as I write, I am perplexed about where to begin. This unnamed woman has been a part of Sunday school lessons, sermons, conference themes, and so forth. We see Jesus as an advocate against those who so easily accuse others and those who consider themselves the custodians of public morality. I have often wondered why this narrative has always been described in the same fashion: *The Adulterous Woman*. For me, several lessons are to be learned, and the one that strikes me as paramount is the action of the men. Why not label this story, *The Hypocrisy of Leaders?* Even today, the focus on adultery continues to disparage this woman. It feels like an unfair heading for a news article used in the tabloids to grab your attention without considering all the facts.

Even as I pored over several resources to hear other voices regarding this woman, I used the word *adultery* and found her easily; however, David's name was omitted. When I searched the word *murderer*, I did not find Moses or David. When I looked up the words *liar* and *deceiver*, I did not find Abraham or Jacob. This one adjective identifies this woman, and the men are seemingly found only by their triumphs. One could argue there is more written about them, which for me stands to reason why their lives should not be told one-dimensionally. I will not belabor this point, but it must be said that as believers, we still have a hard time releasing labels. Unfortunately, this practice has been ingrained in us through the unfortunate choice of those given permission to label freely without thought of the lasting message.

It is also interesting to note that the earliest manuscripts of the canon did not include this passage. It was not until AD 400 when this story was placed in the Gospel of John. There are some scholars who question whether it should be included, but they do not question its authenticity. There are several parallels with stories in the Synoptic Gospels. Some have theorized the inclusion may have been to illustrate John 7:24 and John 8:15 and the Jews' sinfulness compared to Jesus' sinlessness.

So why the choice of this story to use under the sub-heading of Awareness? Sometimes it feels as though we have lost sight of why Jesus came.

Before you push back on this notion, this is the opinion of this lowly author after serving in local, state, and national ministry for over thirty years. We charge so much to WWJD, and it does not resemble him at all. Our focus and our attention seem to get sidetracked by many things that would cause Jesus to go write in the dirt again. God's purpose for sending his Son was to save us. "For God so loved the world..." (John 3:16).

Jesus came to seek and save the lost. How effectively are we sharing this message? Jesus did not run away from sinners but sought fellowship with them. In the three short years of Jesus' ministry, he probably encountered more sinners than what the average church-going, committee-head, morality police will come across in thirty years. Please hear me: this is not a sweeping statement that includes everyone. Unfortunately, it has become the overriding perception of the people who we classify as sinners. Too often, decisions made for the church's good and growth have very little to do with reaching outside the walls. I used to think of ministry with the *Field of Dreams* philosophy: if you build it, they will come. But that is a fantasy movie, and it is a fantasy ministry model.

Jesus' time in the temple was mostly to encourage people to get out of the temple: "Go out to the roads and country lanes and compel them to come" (Luke 14:23). Are we ready to receive them when they arrive? And not just with activities and rules to follow—are our hearts and minds open and ready to embrace with less judgment and more love?

Understanding who the persons were that brought this woman before Jesus also helps to reveal their motives. The Pharisees were a Jewish sect with strict observance of the traditional and written law. They believed themselves to be superior, yet in some ways they made being righteous an easier way. For this group, righteousness could be obtained by certain observances, and this led them to believe they had done everything required of them. Their opinion often put them in conflict with Jesus, for the ethical demand was still present. In one such confrontation, the Pharisees were concerned with the washing of hands before meals. Jesus said, "What goes into someone's mouth does not defile them, but what comes out of their mouth, that is what defiles them" (Matthew 15:11).

Depending on the translation of the Bible, the scribes or teachers of the law accompanied the Pharisees to bring this woman before Jesus. These men exerted power and influence in the religious community. They helped to make judicial conclusions based on scriptural exegesis and were often in conflict with Jesus because he exposed their false exegetical methods.

There is so much abuse of authority against this woman's personhood that it is hard to tell this story. "They made her stand before the group" (v 3) are words that defy respect, compassion, empathy, righteousness, and certainly godly behavior. They brought her to the temple and exposed her in a cruel and harsh manner. She was presented as one who had no rights, stripped of her humanity like a pawn used to make a point or get even. These men's actions were so egregious that we might be tempted to say that such things do not happen today. Oh, but they do. The details may be different, but the lasting scars on the person's soul are the same. When we confront sin, and there are times we must, may we always respond in a manner that, even if someone is found culpable, that person is left with dignity.

The woman was brought before Jesus as a test; they wanted to see how he would respond. It wasn't about her; it was about their discontent with Jesus. There are times when things happen to us seemingly from nowhere. However, all our actions have consequences. Life is an everyday result of reaping what we sow. Therefore, it is so important to live in such a way that our reaping will not bring hurt or disease to our lives and the lives of others. This unnamed woman was going about her life, probably assumingly unnoticed. However, her life choices became the perfect storm for others to use to make an example of her before Jesus and a crowd. I am in no way justifying this woman's sin; we must be held accountable for our choices. Yet while the accusers' motives were questionable, this incident became a transformative event in the lives of everyone involved.

Teacher was a title used to describe one who spoke with authority. The effects of a teacher's words were impressive and brought conviction to those who truly listened. Even Jesus' adversaries had to admit that he taught the way of God objectively, irrespective of the fear or favor of men. So, even though their motives were impure, their acknowledgment of Jesus' identity was quite accurate: "Teacher, this woman was caught in the act of adultery" (v 4).

By law, the act of adultery meant that this woman could be stoned. Being such law-abiding citizens, the Pharisees declared as much to Jesus and demanded that he respond. Not only were they bringing accusations against this woman, but their desire was also to put him in the position to decide contrary to the law. If he agreed to stone her, it would have shown his teachings for compassion and tenderness dealing with sinners to be false. If he let her go, there could have been an upheaval among those who were staunch defenders of the Law handed down by Moses.

Many commentaries detailing this story point out that the absence of the adulterous man is a blatant affront to fairness. If the woman was caught in adultery, why was the man let go? He should have also been present. What they (the Pharisees and scribes) were doing was not meant to be just or fair. The intention was that of men with impure hearts and a desire to be right more than the will to do what was right.

We will never know what Jesus wrote when he bent down and began to write with his finger on the ground. It does not matter; what matters is what he said. Jesus would not allow the Pharisees and scribes to provoke him into anger or speaking out of haste. As they continued to question him, I am sure his silence and seemingly ignoring their questions were even more infuriating for them. When he finally spoke, they were words of clarity, conviction, and compassion even for them: "Let any one of you who is without sin be the first to throw a stone at her" (v 7).

The words of Jesus brought conviction. He did not look at them but spoke with authority and clarity on what they were doing. His gaze was not needed; his words alone carried the weight and power necessary to convey the message. He bent down again and continued to write on the ground after speaking. When he looked up, everyone was gone. They departed from the oldest to the youngest; something touched the heart of everyone present. Could it have been the message and memory of grace?

From the eldest to the youngest, I am sure they were moved, transformed, convicted because of grace and its effects on their lives when they, too, were undeserving. Paul said in 1 Corinthians 15:10, "But by the grace of God I am what I am, and his grace to me was not without effect." Grace is not a one-time event in the Christian experience. We stand in grace; we are empowered by grace. We are recipients of God's unfailing love, his longsuffering, and grace's liberating power. It is easy to understand how the accusers in the group dropped their stones and departed. What Jesus said to them was not found in their list of laws but in life with Christ. Those of us who have lived a little have a longer memory and must be the first to lead others to a better way of living.

Jesus now had an opportunity to stand face-to-face with this woman: from one being accused to another. "Woman, where are they? Has no one condemned you?... Then neither do I condemn you.... Go now and leave your life of sin" (vv 10–11). There was no need for further discussion on the matter. God doesn't rehash and rehearse our past sins. He does not give us permission to seek revenge or recompense, but reminds us, "Therefore, there is now no condemnation for those who are in Christ Jesus, because through Christ Jesus the law of the Spirit who gives life has set you free from the law of sin and death" (Romans 8:1–2).

Go and live, free from sin!

Reflection

I am sure every one of us can recite a time when we felt we were wrongly accused or misunderstood. When the matter was finally cleared up, you were glad it was over. However, if you're honest, you probably wish the resolution had been just as public, but it felt rather anti-climactic. That, my dear, is the way God would have it be. Don't use valuable energy on regret, shame, or wishing the past away, but use the experience as an opportunity to pivot. Allow what God has done to be the central point to readjust, refocus, and rebound. Jesus told Peter how to respond after his denial, after his major disappointment to the cause of Christ: "When you have turned back, strengthen your brothers" (Luke 22:32). Don't rehash what you have done or waste energy; just help someone when you come back to who you were created to be.

Before I share my version of this incident, let me preface this by saying everyone has their side of the story. Even now, as I recall that time, it is with a heart of thanksgiving. I bless God for the outcome and the relationships that formed because of this traumatic time in my life (looking back now, I have lived through worse). I use the word *traumatic* today only because that is how it felt at the time. No, I don't want to relive those moments, but the lessons learned were good. I say this with acceptance of my role in the story; being naïve is not a pass to make mistakes without consequences.

I had been invited to write a six-week Bible study on spiritual gifts before becoming a WCG staff member. The production process for printed resources is typically a year from submission by the writer: editing, proofing, design, and printing. Just as I was joining the staff, the Bible study went into distribution. This was the first time anything I had ever written was in print. I was so excited and sent copies to every family member I could think of, plus a few friends.

The Church of God has taken a stance on many controversial subjects throughout the years, speaking in tongues being one of those. Now let me say, I have been in the Church of God all my life, so I was not unfamiliar with the General Assembly's resolution regarding speaking in tongues. I thought I had been careful to address this area; I even sought input from my pastor and other leaders before submitting my work to the national office.

A year later, while serving as ministry coordinator, I was new to national ministry and a little naïve with no clue or foresight to the things I did not know. I thought everything was going well, and I was finally settling into my role. My speaking engagements and representation on behalf of the ministry were increasing, and I was independently managing my duties. So I was surprised to discover two things: (1) there was a letter circulating among prominent church leaders who took issue with a part of the study, and (2) the part of the study that was problematic had been added by an editor *after* I made my submission. When I saw the letter, the study had already been in circulation for well over a month. Within a week, two speaking engagements suddenly canceled. This may not have been related, but it certainly felt like it was. I was devastated! What had I said that was offensive or contrary to Church of God doctrine? Why didn't those with concerns call me first before drafting and endorsing a letter sent so publicly in the church? Where was living out Matthew 18 before declaring John 8? In other words, if we have a dispute, let us talk about it, one to another, before we publicly choose to shame one another. I was confused, alarmed, and hurt.

I had several meetings on this matter and must admit that a few of those meetings were very disheartening. I was confused because the portion of the Bible study that brought about the controversy, I did not write. I began to feel alone because it appeared no one was coming to my aid. The enemy is amused and glad when we begin to feel isolated, as though no one loves us or understands what we are going through. I pushed against this notion and reached out to the two godly men whom I knew would provide wise counsel and a place of solace. They did not disappoint. They embraced me and counseled me to hold steady and began to make calls on my behalf.

Two occurrences happened during this uproar that changed the course of the attack and changed me and how I approach any written assignment. I believe there are absolutely no coincidences in life; each moment has a purpose. I found myself in the company of someone with influence and understanding of both sides of this situation. She questioned me about my role and tried to help me understand why there was so much concern. Here is an excerpt from the letter:

> It is our considered opinion that this lesson not only is inconsistent with the traditional Church of God teaching and doctrine, but it is also in contradiction of the 1987 Resolution on Speaking in Tongues passed by the General Assembly of the Church of God meeting in Anderson, Indiana in June of that year.

When I told her that I had not written the part that was in question, she immediately advised me on the next steps. First, I needed to clarify that I was not the author of that portion of the study and that it was included after submission. The second occurrence was a tender accountability meeting with Dr. Gil Stafford. Professor Stafford may not be with us anymore, but his teachings and counsel left an indelible mark on my life beyond this event. Dr. Stafford gently but firmly said to me when I went to him for advice as the dust was settling, "Arnetta, do not ever allow anyone to add to your writing without your permission."

I take responsibility for my part in this unfortunate situation. Being naïve and excited to have my work published was a formula ready-made for something like this to occur. I did not ask enough questions and accepted a process unfamiliar to me without regard for its outcome. Yes, I was angry, disillusioned, and hurt for a period. I contemplated whether I wanted to continue to serve. I allowed that thinking to last briefly. It was non-productive and certainly not God's will. I was now aware of what I needed to know, and I moved on.

The lessons learned and the relationships established have far outweighed what the enemy tried to do to thwart God's purpose for my being at the Women of the Church of God. I was determined not to let this event distract from or distort the work God had prepared in advance for me to do. Had I walked away in the early 2000s, I would have missed all the amazing things God did. It was not in vain.

Often when we want to bring or raise awareness to something, it is with great fanfare: big campaigns, committees formed, educational and social events planned. Under normal circumstances, these strategies would work, but here Jesus was teaching Kingdom principles. He raised awareness of the weakness of the Law alone being the moral compass to righteousness. The first thing I noticed in the story was how Jesus kept his *composure*. He desired to speak to their hearts and not their head knowledge. No matter what the Pharisees and the teachers of the law did, Jesus remained calm. When life is pressing in and people are against us, our natural response is to react to the pressure. We want to defend ourselves and make it public. However, our will not only influences our state of mind, it's a testimony of our faith. William J. Toms reportedly said, "Be careful how you live; you will be the only Bible some people will ever read."

When Mary of Bethany sat at Jesus' feet, her sister, Martha, complained about Mary's lack of assistance. Again, Jesus, being our advocate, said, "Mary has chosen what is better, and it will not be taken away from her" (Luke 10:42). When Stephen was being stoned for his faith, he responded calmly by praying on behalf of his accusers. Saul was standing there watching. How much do you think Stephen's actions influenced Saul's response on the road to Damascus?

Never walk in the chaos of your accusers. With calm assurance, walk boldly in the truth that you were created in the image of God and his likeness. God will take us through something to bring awareness to the accusers for their well-being also. Every soul is important; they, too, are his creation!

Notice the composure of the woman also. She stood silently, but there's no mention of her head bowed or her speaking up in her defense. We should never add to Scripture what is not there, but we can only imagine. Had she resolved that because she was guilty, there was no need to try to defend herself? Maybe she, too, knew who Jesus was. She had heard of his teachings and his compassion for sinners, and perhaps Jesus would speak on her behalf. Her sin of being adulterous did not mean that there was no good in her at all; there was more to who she was. Maybe at that moment, she knew her future could be greater than her sin. There was something about this woman's silence and composure that seemed to say, "I am in the presence of Jesus, the one who can speak to the winds and the waves, and they obey his will."

There are times when we try to fix a situation, and we just make matters worse. Psalms 46 tells us, "God is our refuge and strength, an ever-present help in trouble" (v 1). The chapter goes on to say, "Be still, and know that I am God" (v 10). We can stay calm when we believe, even in the midst of our troubles, that God has not abandoned us. Find God in self-control! Whatever you may be facing at this moment that seems insurmountable, that is where God is. He works in our impossible. I heard a preacher once say, "When you are in over your head, you are exactly where God wants you to be." Ladies, there are times when our greatest weapon to solve our problem is found in our serenity in and dependency on God.

In my story, my help came when I ceased trying to fix it. It was in those moments that an accidental meeting occurred which brought change. Even though I wanted to shout from the rooftop what I felt was an injustice, I also knew it was vital how I handled myself during this crisis. In the last few years, I have been privileged to invite others to write on behalf of the ministry. Because of my experience, I am sensitive to the submissions provided by the writers. We seek to be always diligent in giving each writer final approval before publication.

Did this unnamed woman keep her composure because she knew she stood before the very one who was sent to become her advocate, her *champion*? We are desperately held captive by sin and needed a defender: "For God so loved the world that he gave his one and only Son" (John 3:16).

Jesus, our champion, affirmed this woman's right to be treated fairly and just and the freedom to live her life with access to the same benefits afforded her accusers. I love the visual of Jesus rooting us on, in the bleachers of our life, encouraging us to keep going; you can make it.

The notion that we were created to be failures or not have success goes against the very nature of who God is. Mistakes happen. Situations occur in life that are uncomfortable, some from our own doing and others created to stand in our way and defeat us. We were created to do good works, which God has prepared in advance for us to do. What will happen if we allow those who stand against us to distract us from the purpose of God? Yes, the thought of running may occur, but I encourage you to stay in the fray and fight. "If God is for us, who can be against us?" (Romans 8:31).

Why do you think the enemy has worked overtime trying to get you off course? He wants you to hang your head in defeat.

What I love so much about this story is that this woman and Jesus were the last two standing. She stood through all of this. Yes, she had sinned, but there was a determination in her to stay strong. She stood long enough to hear Jesus speak, and she believed. With the help of the Holy Spirit, she believed that she could leave the temple with her head held high, walking in the fullness of who God purposed her to be.

Keep moving; someone is waiting to hear your victory story. Can you imagine the story this woman shared and the lives transformed? If Jesus did it for her, he can do it for me.

Other women who may have been in similar situations are watching from the sidelines to see what will happen. They, too, need a champion, someone who will fight for them and even die that they might live.

My sister, someone is in the shadows of your life, looking on, watching you as you have met your hills and valleys and kept running. We often refer to Hebrews 12:1–2 in reference to saints who have gone before us, rooting for us from heaven to keep the faith: "Therefore, since we are surrounded by such a great cloud of witnesses, let us throw off everything that hinders and the sin that so easily entangles. And let us run with perseverance the race marked out for us, fixing our eyes on Jesus, the pioneer and perfecter of faith." I would like to think this passage applies to those we encounter each day, those who are faithful and understand the journey, those who have been watching how we live, how we react, how we hold on when it seems all hope is gone. These people understand your struggles, and they are rooting for you to throw off the weight, the things that have tried to stop you. They are cheering for you to finish strong, so you, too, can become a part of the huge crowd of witnesses. They get it because they, also, have been championed by God.

The final act in this brief story is when Jesus said to the woman, "Go, and sin no more" (v 11, KJV). There are times when a simple phrase is all we need. Stop the sin; don't return to your old habits. His command did not stop there. He gave a word of hope: go, *continue*, resume your life.

Continue, don't let challenges interrupt what you were doing. Let them be the fuel to keep you going and reignite your passion. Move forward with a new resolve. An old Church of God hymn says, "God sets [the church's] members each in place, according to his will."[5] Your crisis, this traumatic moment in your life, may have drawn attention to you, but make the most of it. Be aware that this is your opportunity, and what you do next is key. For some, this will be the first point of reference to who you are; live it in such a way that brings good to the body and glory to God.

Someone may be in a holding pattern. Maybe a crisis, hurt, sickness, misunderstanding, opposition, disappointment, or fear has caused you to stop. You may question, "Why go further; who cares?" Jesus and the people waiting for the services you have been ordained and set apart to provide do. Get up, dust yourself off, take off the big t-shirt, and get back to work. I know it's not easy but press your way through. It's worth it.

When the disciples didn't believe Mary Magdalene had seen the risen Savior, she could have let that stop her, but she continued on her mission. She had been a recipient of God's great salvation when Jesus delivered her from seven demonic spirits. She followed him all the way to the cross. Her gratitude did not end there; she was there at dawn the first day of the week. At first, she didn't realize it was Jesus until he called her by name. "Mary.... Do not hold on to me.... Go instead to my brothers and tell them, 'I am ascending to my Father and your Father, to my God and your God' " (John 20:16–17). Mary was obedient; she went and told the disciples, "I have seen the Lord!" (John 20:18).

Continue; this is not the end. There is not a period in your life; there is more to your story. There are chapters still unfolding and a cause that is beckoning you to lend your voice and your stories of victory.

Conclusion

Wake up church, women's groups, and auxiliaries! Be aware: there are sinners among us—those who have made mistakes and probably those currently struggling. Don't let them stand in the temple alone. Stand with them, "for all have sinned and fall short of the glory of God" (Romans 3:23). But we have a champion, and his name is Jesus!

5 Charles W. Naylor, "O Church of God," *Worship the Lord: Hymnal of the Church of God* (Anderson, IN: Warner Press, 1989), 289.

Questions for Reflection

1. Are you in a holding pattern? If so, how can you release whatever is causing it, knowing that God your pilot is ready to take off?
2. Jesus is our champion! Whom do you need to champion to aid to the next level?
3. Never walk in the chaos of your accuser! How will you handle the next attack, because it's coming?

PART 3

God's Presence

CHAPTER 7

God Sees Us!

"So do not fear, for I am with you; do not be dismayed, for I am your God. I will strengthen you and help you; I will uphold you with my righteous right hand." —Isaiah 41:10

The prophet Isaiah was writing this message, this prophetic word beforehand, to comfort the people of God who would be taken into exile. These words were spoken to encourage the Jews on how to live and respond toward the end of their seventy years of captivity. As they prepared to leave, Isaiah's words were given as a reminder that whether it was the past, future, or current day, God was still very aware of their suffering.

Although this is an Old Testament scripture, its meaning and promises are eternal. The Lord is Immanuel, and he has established a covenant with his people. God will graciously deliver and vindicate his chosen people. He will also establish order by his power. God sees the steps of our lives and gets involved in the minutiae. He is not far off but very present. We can take comfort in knowing he came to this world amongst humanity to deliver us from sin and dwell with us in our suffering.

I enjoyed my time as ministry coordinator. It afforded me the opportunity to do what I love doing—working with women and dreaming of ways to help equip, empower, and enable groups to serve globally. In that role, I did not have to worry or be concerned about finances. I had the luxury of sitting in board meetings, attentive but not burdened by structural and sustainability issues. That luxury ended abruptly when I became executive director.

I remember one night seeking the Lord for direction and answers when he took me to Jeremiah 1:17, "Get yourself ready! Stand up and say to them whatever I command you. Do not be terrified by them." I lived and feasted on this verse for several months. For a shy person to be told to get ready to speak with authority was daunting. I would soon discover that trouble was looming, and I needed confidence from God to lead through these turbulent times.

When the Lord gave me the words from Jeremiah, it was a prophetic message. Nothing had yet occurred; however, in preparation for what God knew was coming, I had been alerted to ready myself, speak the words given to me from God, and not be afraid. God sees what is ahead with all its rewards and dangers. "The eyes of the LORD are everywhere, keeping watch on the wicked and the good" (Proverbs 15:3).

Hagar: Assurance in God Alone

Genesis 16; 21:8–20

I must note the difficulty as an African American woman to engage this story from a historical point of view and not deal with the racial and barbaric implications of how this woman was treated. That will be the next book. Hagar's status in society was so low that she was required by law at the whim and notion of another to engage in sexual relations whether she wanted to or not. When she was no longer pleasing, she could—and was—cast out. Most commentaries today have found justification in this activity. I accept that it was the norm of ancient day, but it still screams loud in my spirit to address the abuse, injustice, and lack of respect for another person. The patriarchs believed and accepted the story of God's creation of the heavens and the earth. How then did they reconcile male and female, made in the image of God and his likeness, with conceiving, condoning, and following customs that are contrary to God's plan for humankind? Thank God for Jesus!

My personal feelings aside, we must celebrate the strength, resilience, and courage of this woman. We are charged to shed more light on who she was; we cannot accept the voices who still justify and lend a word of sympathy to her abusers. This may have been what some recite as the "norm," but it doesn't make it right or acceptable. In my retelling of this story, I pray that I accurately interpret the text and lend another perspective. Hagar was an awe-inspiring woman, then and now!

There are so many lessons that one can glean from the life of Hagar in an in-depth character study. This was the first angelic visit from heaven to a woman recorded in Scripture. Hagar stands before us in the very notable rank of faith, trust, and assurance. She stands with a select few individuals who had a close, face-to-face fellowship with God. With seemingly no control over her life, this bondswoman was one of the few whom God chose to speak with personally.

Hagar is an Egyptian name. The Bible provides no record of her genealogy; researchers have surmised that she was a slave and possibly given to Abram and Sarai by Pharaoh when they visited Egypt. Slavery is dehumanizing then and now, in any era. This young woman was not only the property of Abram and Sarai, but she would also now be used for the gain of this couple with no thought of how this act would affect her as a person. Ishmael, the son Hagar bore for Abram, began the tribe of the Ishmaelites. They would later be the Arab people from whom came Mohammed, the founder of Islam.

When the story begins, Sarai and Abram were still without an heir, waiting anxiously for the promise of God to be fulfilled that "a son who is your own flesh and blood will be your heir" (Genesis 15:4). Being concerned, probably because of their age, Sarai decided to take matters into her own hands. She offered her slave girl to Abram so that their family line would continue. Surrogacy was not an uncommon practice in the ancient Near East. It was a woman's duty to supply her husband with an heir. When she could not, she would offer her maidservant as a surrogate. The child born from this liaison was the legal heir of this couple.

Can you imagine how alone and helpless Hagar must have felt at that moment? Here she finds herself a part of a nomadic group traveling further and further away from her home. Her ethnicity and traditions brought another level of separation. Her dark-skinned complexion and practice of worshiping the sun and moon as deities probably did not endear her to her neighbors. This chasm between the two women was an indicator of how desperate Sarai had to be to conceive such a notion. It is not that God will not use our differences to make us one, but the elements of this union were certainly not in line with God's promise to Abram to bring forth an heir that would be their flesh and blood.

The attempt to secure the child of promise through Hagar was a lack of faith by Sarai and Abram. Their actions produced years of suffering and tears on both sides. Sarai would later declare to Abram, "You are responsible for the wrong I am suffering. I put my slave in your arms, and now that she knows she is pregnant, she despises me. May the Lord judge between you and me" (Genesis 16:5). Had she asked for the judgment of the Lord beforehand, they would not have been in this predicament.

Hagar began to look upon Sarai with displeasure. Was she angry because her choices had been taken away? Was she feeling a sense of power because she was pregnant by the master? Was she being ridiculed by others because of jealousy? As a surrogate, was she feeling the stirrings of this child, her son, growing inside of her, knowing that when he was born, she had no legal right to him? We will never know the reason for her emotions, but it is clear they ran deep. Hagar would complicate matters further by showing dishonor to her mistress.

Strife quickly followed the unfortunate act playing out between these three individuals. It is easy to look from the outside and say, "Turn the other cheek." When people come against us and say and do all manner of evil against us, how do we shake it off? Because this couple became impatient, not believing that the all-sufficient God could still perform his promise at any age, they took matters into their own hands. What happened was the blame game. There was surely enough blame to go around, but let's be clear: the one who suffered the most was the bondwoman, even though the problem created did not originate with her.

One can only ask the question today, why didn't Abram take a stance to bring a resolution? Here was a husband seemingly desperate to make his wife happy and avoid conflict. Hagar's position had been elevated to the second wife when given to Abram by Sarai. Nevertheless, here we see Abram refer to her as a servant. He gave Sarai permission to do whatever she thought was best. In the original Hebrew, the more exacting translation for what occurred is that Sarai humbled her. Sarai reduced Hagar back to her original condition by dealing with her harshly.

Hagar ran away! As a bondswoman, she was the property of Sarai and was forbidden to leave without permission, no matter how unkind the treatment. She was in violation of cultural laws and was considered a runaway slave. It was not a convoy sent to retrieve Hagar that found her, but the angel of the Lord. God sees you when others don't. When you feel stripped of your personhood as a means to an end, when your freedom to decide has been taken away from you—God is in those situations.

As Hagar fled in desperation, she stopped at a spring in the desert of Shur. She was on the road that led back to Egypt. Hagar was going back home, looking for her freedom. I remember when I first heard this story and the disappointment I felt when the angel told her she had to go back. What? Why should she submit herself to these attacks? My question was the very reason for her to return, the act of submission.

The angel of the Lord said to her, "Hagar, slave of Sarai, where have you come from, and where are you going?" (Genesis 16:8). Clearly he knew where she was coming from, but he needed her to articulate where she was going. "I am running away from my mistress" (v 8). How many of us have felt the same as Hagar? How many of us have thought, "I am out! I do not have to put up with this treatment!" There are moments of retreat that God sanctions. This was not that moment. Running at times is contrary to God's divine purpose for that situation. Elijah ran and tried to hide out in a cave. God sent him back. Why? Because his assignment was not complete. He needed to prepare his successor. Going back into a tough situation is a sign of strength and commitment to complete the task.

God had a plan for Hagar, and for the moment, it was not to escape. The thought of returning to what clearly was a degrading situation was accompanied by a promise. This was a personal message of hope for Hagar from God. He was coming alongside her. God was going to bless her with a son. Having a son was very significant in ancient times. She was alone in a foreign land with no social status or security to fall back on. God's promise included not only a son but also a multitude of descendants to care for her when she was old.

When we look from the literal standpoint of God's promise to Hagar, it seems rather discouraging: "He will be a wild donkey of man; his hand will be against everyone" (v 12). In the ancient world, wild donkeys expressed freedom and independence. I believe what Hagar heard was that this son would remain independent of people around him who would like to overpower him. For a woman living under constraints, this was a message of hope, one of liberation and freedom for her family. Even if it would take years for its manifestation, she knew the day would come.

Hagar was to return and submit to Sarai, to follow Sarai's instructions and accept her place as the bondswoman and mistress. Attached to this command was a promise, a covenant between her and God that she was not forsaken. Accepting what we know will bring difficulty and strife in obedience to God always reaps benefits. Hagar's act of submitting to Sarai was not about Sarai's authority over her life but about Hagar trusting God's power over the situation.

Submission is a spiritual principle; it is a divine work. Submission teaches self-discipline. It is putting aside our own desires for the benefit of others and not always doing what you want to do. Clearly, Hagar struggled in that area because of her unproductive behavior toward Sarai. She could not improve her station by disrespecting her mistress. She was unleashing the power of God's promise to manifest itself in her life. Go back; the son you are carrying will carry you into your future.

It was in this moment, being in the presence of God, that Hagar found strength to endure. Her promise, though filled with splendor and significance, would have pain and conflict.

While Ishmael, the son Hagar carried, would produce offspring too numerous to count, he also would live in hostility toward his brothers. Her return to Sarai was preparation for how to live and manage a life of conflict. God has a way of offering hope with realistic expectations. I love the way Paul explained life in 2 Corinthians 4: "We are hard pressed on every side, but not crushed; perplexed, but not in despair; persecuted, but not abandoned; struck down, but not destroyed" (vv 8–9).

Hagar came from a land of gods, but in this moment she was influenced by what she had seen and heard from Abram and the people around her. She knew this was the one true God. Her words of recognition gave her the resolve to return: "I have now seen the One who sees me" (v 13). As she turned to go back, she stopped long enough at the well—*Beer Lahai Roi*: the well of him who lives and sees me—then she departed. When Hagar's son was born she named him Ishmael, meaning "God hears."

For fifteen years, it appears as though they all lived in peace. There is no mention of continued strife until after Isaac was born. Isaac was weaned around the age of three, and a great feast was given in his honor. Ishmael began to mock the child. Sarah said to Abraham, "Get rid of that slave woman and her son, for that woman's son will never share in the inheritance with my son Isaac" (Genesis 21:10). No mother will stand by and allow her child to be mistreated.

Abraham, now fond of both sons, was distraught by the news. However, God assured him that Ishmael, though not the child of the covenant, would be okay: "I will make the son of the slave into a nation also, because he is your offspring" (v 13). The next morning, Abraham sent them away with some food and a skin of water. The two traveled in the desert of Beersheba. After the water was gone, Hagar put Ishmael under a bush and sat opposite him—close enough to be in earshot, but out of her sight, for she could not bear to see him die.

Ishmael began to cry and, once again, Hagar had a heavenly visit: "What is the matter, Hagar? Do not be afraid; God has heard the boy crying as he lies there. Lift the boy up and take him by the hand, for I will make him into a great nation" (Genesis 21:17–18).

Reflection

Charles Dickens's *A Tale of Two Cities* begins with the phrase, "It was the best of times, it was the worst of times." Life is filled with contrast. God is at work in our suffering and our spiritual advantages. He works in our anxiety to exalt himself; our troubles will show his triumph, and on the other side of our incredible sadness is the salvation of the Lord.

My service to Women of the Church of God has been one of the most rewarding ministry assignments of my life. When I look back, if I had asked God to design an opportunity for me to serve that was tailor-made for me, this would be the one. No, I didn't come with all the skills necessary to be successful in the job, but I came believing God and surrounding myself with people who were more skilled in my areas of weakness and seeking their counsel.

In year one, I realized the ministry was facing a financial crisis. Jeff Jenness, serving at the time as director of the Board of Pensions, which would later become Servant Solutions, came to my aid in profound ways. I knew how to balance a checkbook, but I had little understanding of a balance sheet. The second year, we faced a breach of trust that had been ongoing before my arrival. The only recourse was the transparency of our discovery with the larger body. The decision to be open was easy, and the response across the movement was swift and diverse. There were those who were compassionate, others disappointed, a few leery of our leadership but overall grateful that we were open and honest and remained so until the matter was settled.

While serving as ministry coordinator, I remember the major overhaul of our database. As I transitioned to executive director faced with the responsibility of dealing with this overhaul and the crisis, I remember praying, *God, please do not let the ministry dissolve under my leadership.* Our database for membership told a challenging story: in 1982 we had 40,000 members; in 1992 membership was 30,000; in 2003 it was 16,500.

When we performed this major database overhaul in 2003, we recognized that the data had not been purged in many years, so the numbers prior to the cleanup were not accurate. However, the membership decline was still evident. As we labored with this information, we could see that we had maybe five years left at most, then the doors would be closed. I refused to accept this outcome. I believed in our God who sees and remembers his promises. I didn't know how we would do it; I had no place else to go but my faith in God.

Recognizing a need for a paradigm shift, we proposed to the WCG Board of Directors in the fall of 2007 to conduct a survey of pastors, pastors' wives, women involved with WCG, women not participating, and focus groups. We enlisted the services of Dr. Michael D. Wiese who suggested the title Relevance Survey, and the process began. The resulting comprehensive sixty-page report was concluded and presented to the Board in September 2008.

The results included the following: (1) Pastors believed the Women of the Church of God was outdated. They believed in *what* we were doing, but the *how* was in question. (2) Missions was still very important to the church, but how it was presented needed to be restructured. (3) Women's ministry was now becoming a major part of local congregations with greater fluidity and fewer cookie-cutter methods. (4) Finally, the hardest truth for our loyal and faithful members to accept, we were seen as a clique. Suggestions for sustainability were provided as well: (1) Change your name was the first reply across the board. (2) Re-brand your approach to missions. (3) Create an environment that is inclusive for all women. (4) Be a resource for women's ministry.

Che-Che Mobley followed Laura Shallenberger as president of the Board of Directors during this survey process. Both of us, being new to our positions when this survey was completed, engaged in many long conversations regarding the future of WCG. We had the opportunity to travel to Uganda together and talked our way across the Atlantic Ocean. Filled with hopes and dreams for the future and armed with the data from the Relevance Survey, we asked ourselves what was next. How should we interpret what we already knew?

Born out of the trip was a renewed sense of purpose and direction. When we returned to the United States, we knew change was on the horizon. Che-Che posed the question we were asking ourselves as recorded in *An Unfinished Agenda*: "Were we in the business of increasing the membership for Christian Women Connection/Women of the Church of God, or were we interested in making disciples, raising up godly women, and helping women discover more of the presence of God? Reaching those women would necessitate the development of new methods and ministries that would prevent the demise of the ministry."[6]

How does this story align with Hagar's story? We have lived with the assurance that God saw us and cared about us. Every step of the journey, God has been there. When others could no longer see who we were, God saw us. He also encouraged us to stay the course when we wanted to run away and abandon the ship. We were charged to build stronger alliances, submit to the needs of the people we were called to serve, and trust God for the increase.

This story is a reminder that God sees our *plight*. He is very aware of our troubles, what we are going through. The smallest details of life, God knows. He said to the Israelites, "I have indeed seen the misery of my people in Egypt. I have heard them crying out because of their slave drivers, and I am concerned about their suffering" (Exodus 3:7). Suffering is not easy, but we can endure when we know we live in the sight of God. As believers, we understand that God is actively at work through our tribulation.

Let go of your poor self-image. God sees you. We are not invisible to God. Hagar said, "I have...seen the One who sees me" (Genesis 16:13). What happens to us matters to God. Because of mistreatment, rejection, criticism, failures, and other forms of hurt and pain, we have a low opinion of ourselves. We view life in this absolute and begin to question if God's love for others is greater than his love for us. God loves us with an *everlasting love* and will protect and care for us even when we are unaware.

Yes, there are times when we want God to fix this *now!* We don't want to suffer any longer. However, it is during those times when we witness the sufficiency of God's grace toward us. He has not abandoned us, not at all. It is during those times when we recognize the reason we made it Remember the story when Jesus spoke to the winds and waves? Mark is the only Gospel that records, "Leaving the crowd behind, they took him along, just as he was, in the boat. There were also other boats with him" (4:36). We have heard many sermons and lessons taught about Jesus' response to the disciples and how he stilled the wind and the waves. The storm that faced the disciples was the same storm facing the smaller, less

6 Che-Che Mobley, *An Unfinished Agenda* (Anderson, IN: Warner Press, 2013), 178.

noticeable boats—the ones that were seemingly so insignificant that only one writer recorded their presence. However, these individuals were faced with the same plight; who saw them? God did! When Jesus spoke to the winds and the waves, it included even them.

At times many of us have felt like the *other boats*, like our status or station in life causes people to overlook us and the problems we face. Maybe because you are not the main story, it feels as if no one is listening to your story. Is it a situation where you can't offer what the larger, more prominent ministries can offer, so you feel dismissed? Maybe your resources are not as vast as they used to be, but you are still rowing along. In the scheme of things, you too have difficulty, but in comparison, you feel overlooked. You are not invisible or unrecognized before God; he sees you and the dilemma also. Hold on to your faith.

The list of unwanted circumstances that come into our lives may seem long. God is not random in his actions. There is always a purpose for what he does. God will use the worst of conditions to further that purpose. When life hurts, and it will, what is God saying and doing? When I look back now at a few of the ministry's tough years, I have no explanation of why we made it. My only response is that God saw our plight and he was actively engaged in every moment.

God sees our plight, and he guides our *path*. If we let him, he will lead the way. I said earlier how disappointed I was in the angel to order Hagar to return, especially after hearing the rest of the story. Hagar left a second and final time. However, the second time she did not run away; she was sent away. Why then did God bring her back into the situation when, ultimately, she ended up leaving again? Because his purpose, which included not only Hagar but also Sarai and Abram, was not complete.

Hagar was required by God to return home to what appeared to be an impossible living arrangement. She was obedient, and for fifteen years she remained stable in her environment. Scripture is silent regarding Hagar until after Isaac is born. Was the relationship peaceful between her and Sarai? Whatever the case may have been, the Lord protected and cared for her and Ishmael until he turned fourteen years old.

Jeremiah 29:11 is often used out of context as a security blanket. We use it to imply that we have an escape from our troubles, but that is not so.

The meaning of this verse in context is to help us see that we can also thrive in our suffering. The Israelites were in exile, and Jeremiah wanted to confront a false prophet, Hananiah, who had claimed that God would free them from Babylon in two years. Yes, God would fulfill his promise, but after seventy years. In the meantime, they had to live in peace with their captors and pray for their prosperity. Why? Because if the captors prospered, so then would they. God's will was being perfected, but not through the actions of a genie in a bottle.

Hagar was told she had to go back, submit, and live in peace; while with Abraham she witnessed prosperity, numerically and monetarily. Our best season of development comes through perseverance and not our escape. Now the quote from Jeremiah fits: " 'For I know the plans I have for you,' declares the LORD, 'plans to prosper you and not to harm you, plans to give you hope and a future' " (Jeremiah 29:11). It sheds a whole new light on the lessons learned in our suffering.

When Isaac was born, Ishmael mocked the child, and Ishmael and Hagar were banished from their home. Even as they left on an uncertain path, God was yet aware of their circumstances. They left with less than what one would expect since Ishmael was Abram's son, but Hagar was walking the path set before her. This mother, seemingly broken and defeated when the water was gone, sat down in despair, with her back turned away from her child. She was not out of earshot if he needed her, but she was unable to watch him die. After all, he was the child on behalf of whom God had spoken a promise. How confusing this time had to be for Hagar! The events occurring before her on that day did not match the words spoken to her fifteen years prior.

As Ishmael cried in distress, the meaning of his name reached the ears of heaven. Hagar had chosen to walk the path God had designed for her. Subverting her will and submitting to direction from God was not easy. Her choosing the path and directions from God happened when she returned home, and so did the chosen name for her child, "God hears."

Hagar was now on her own. The angel did not charge her to return; instead, he said, "Lift the boy up and take him by the hand, for I will make him into a great nation" (Genesis 21:18). This ending feels almost like Abram's conversation with God after Lot, his nephew, had departed from him. When the Lord told Abram to leave his country and all that he had known, God was specific in his directions and his covenant. However,

Abram took Lot with him. In most translations of Scripture, Lot's coming seems like Abram's idea and not God's. After many years of prosperity and arguments, Abram decided it best to separate from Lot. Immediately after Lot departed, the Lord said, "Look around from where you are, to the north and south, to the east and west. All the land that you see I will give to you and your offspring" (Genesis 13:14–15).

After Hagar had left the company of Abraham and Sarah at the appointed time, she saw the promise fulfilled. The first time, she was running away; the second time, she was sent away. Hagar, this poor Egyptian slave girl, birthed a nation.

"Show me your ways, Lord, teach me your paths" (Psalm 25:4). I remember when Che-Che and I were faced with the question about which way to choose. Survey aside, God showed us which way to go. It happened on an Immersion trip in 2008 to Uganda and Kenya. Unbeknownst to us, the Lord had prepared this on a continent far from home as the place for us to hear his voice.

We attended the Church of God Women's Convention held in Uganda at the Kasubi headquarters of the Church of God compound in Kampala. (I was blessed to build long-standing relations from that meeting that are still a part of my life today.) The delegates in attendance were from Congo, Rwanda, Sudan, and Kenya. During our visit, we traveled to many rural villages to see firsthand how the animal project and grandmother project were impacting the communities. We also visited many clinics, one in particular served by missionary Glenna Phippen. This was our first introduction to the Tumaini AIDS Prevention Program (TAPP). In this ministry, beautiful jewelry was made to help support the women and their families suffering from this disease. We saw God at work in marvelous ways, but we also were touched by the vastness of unmet needs.

The women leaders in Africa wanted to meet with us after one evening service to share our *expertise* in women's ministry. When I look back on this, I realize how interesting this request was. We were fortunate to have several members of the board of directors as a part of the team. We divided up our presentation and worked diligently the night before on what to share. One by one, we stood and highlighted the different projects sponsored by Women of the Church of God. We were happy to share about the various fund campaigns designated to raise dollars for missions. They listened intently for well over an hour. Then very humbly, Beatrice Abasoola raised her hand to speak. These seven words still challenge me today. She simply said, "But how do you spread the gospel?" One person spoke and began to reiterate our funding ideas and how we raise dollars for distribution to help missionaries and the projects designed through their efforts. She looked at us tenderly, and we recognized that, in that moment, God was showing us a new path. We ended up being more influenced by their work than they were by ours.

The spreading of the gospel most certainly can be a collective effort. Yes, it takes resources, dollars, and commitment from others to reach all the places we can't physically go but have a need. However, what this dear woman said to us was a personal challenge. "How do *you* spread the gospel...? The concept of missions to Sister Beatrice included the spreading of the gospel *within her own community*. Therefore, if that is the true concept of missions, then the vision and emphasis of Women of the Church of God must include spreading the gospel and ministering to women in the United States as well as in other countries. The truth is that ministering locally authenticates missions in foreign lands."[7]

Che-Che and I looked at each other and knew the Lord had spoken. We have never lost sight of our role and our commitment to supporting our missionaries, but we also saw that we were called as part of Jesus' disciples, charged to *go and make disciples*.

Not everyone will understand when you choose the path God has carved out for you. It also is often not the easiest road. Expect to be confronted, challenged, and maybe even ridiculed. However, whatever you do, keep trusting God through it all. It was during the early years following this expansion of ministry focus that I better understood Jeremiah 1:17: "Get yourself ready! Stand up and say to them whatever I command you. Do not be terrified by them."

Is this rebranding holy? This was a question that was posed to me in 2010. That year we changed our name for the fifth time since 1932 to what is now known as Christian Women Connection. I asked Che-Che in 2012 if she would consider writing our story from where *Madame President* left off in 1974 to the present day. Historically, we know that our story will be told, so why not tell it from our vantage point without interpretation?

---

7 Che-Che Mobley, *An Unfinished Agenda* (Anderson, IN: Warner Press, 2013), 174.

Yes, we lost local groups who felt we had abandoned missions, but, praise God, we gained groups who believed in what we were doing. In ten years, we have seen a numerical growth of more than eight thousand new partners, twenty-five new groups, and resources that address relevant issues for today with missions support still intact.

When we follow God's path for our lives, he will then *perfect* that plan. I am sure that Hagar's suffering was not over. However, the God who sees allowed her to see her future. Psalm 138:8 says, "The LORD will perfect *that which* concerns me" (NKJV). *Perfect* means he will bring things to completion. Concerns are those things that make us anxious or cause us to worry. Worry can have a positive side that can move you into action, or it can turn your faith into fear. Whatever you do, keep moving. You, dear one, are in the presence of the God who hears you and rest assured, he sees your going out and coming in.

Conclusion

An old hymn by John W. Peterson says: "It's not an easy road we are trav'ling to Heaven."[8] The hymn goes on to talk about the difficulties on the road to heaven, but the promise that Jesus is with us. His presence gives us joy through trial, trouble, and danger, and he smooths out the path for us.

Questions for Reflection

1. God can use the worst of conditions to further his purposes. Hagar was in a crisis that was out of her control, and it catapulted her into a new season. God did not abandon her. He cared for, protected, provided for, and blessed her. How has God provided and blessed you through a crisis?

2. As you look through your life and ministry, think of a crisis out of your control that catapulted you into an overhaul of your vision and mission. How did you experience a renewed sense of direction?

3. "Is this rebranding holy?" How have you had to "rebrand" a part of your life, ministry, or mission to be relevant in a newly sensed purpose?

8 John W. Peterson, "It's Not an Easy Road," *Hymns of Faith* (Tabernacle Publishing, 1980), 414.

CHAPTER 8

God Hears Us!

This is the confidence we have in approaching God: that if we ask anything according to his will, he hears us. And if we know that he hears us—whatever we ask—we know that we have what we asked of him.
—1 John 5:14–15

There is great comfort in knowing that God listens to his children and his judgment is always according to truth. It is his desire, as Scripture reminds us, to give us "good gifts." The beginning of our petition must be rooted in our relationship with God. The sum of Christian knowledge is that our life is in Christ and our will and desires will align themselves with our request that everything be according to his will. When this happens, God's ear is open and ever attentive.

Our prayer is granted in the best manner and will promote our good. As believers we can have confidence that what we ask God for is not disregarded, whether it is answered immediately or over time. What is bestowed upon us is for our good; it may not be what we asked for specifically, but it will be what we need.

As a child I remember having dreams of having children. I even had names and sexes picked out. I came from a large family, thirteen children total, and my dreams were *big*. I believe my longing was impacted greatly by my mother. She loved us well, individually and as a unit. She passed when I was in my early twenties, but she left me with a heart filled with memories, godly wisdom, timely advice, and prophetic words to last a lifetime.

I recognize that the desire to have children is not every woman's desire, and that's okay, but each one of us has desired something—a yearning so deep that you cannot imagine life without it. What happens when we are given an alternate answer? Did God hear us? Yes, he did. How do we faithfully live each day with a healthy acceptance of God's will?

Hannah: A Favored Life

1 Samuel 1:1—2:21

Hannah was a prophetess whose name, in Hebrew, meant *favor* or *grace*. She carried a burden for her people and an unfulfilled longing. The backdrop of this story is a time when the priests were corrupt, and Israel was at a low point spiritually. This pious woman's longing was to please God and have children. Hannah's life was an example of how to live in peace while waiting patiently for a prayer to be answered. This type of holding pattern may be filled with moments of frustration, yet during those times, God's desire is to teach us and reach us while we wait.

Hannah was one of two wives married to Elkanah. In the Old Testament, it was common for men to have multiple wives. Penninah was the other wife of Elkanah, and she had borne him children. Hannah was barren. In ancient Israel, children were considered a clear sign of God's blessing, especially sons. The inability of a Jewish woman to conceive brought disgrace and great suffering. Infertility meant she was unable to fulfill her God-given purpose of procreation. It was seen as a failure to fulfill her primary role in the family. Life is bad enough when we feel as though we have failed, but when that failure is on public display, it can be devastating.

Although Hannah was barren, she was loved the most by her husband. Elkanah was a Zuphite from the hill country of Ephraim; he adored Hannah. Every year they traveled to Shiloh to offer sacrifice to God. Hophni and Phinehas were Eli's sons serving as priests. Their story of corruption becomes more prominent as the story of Samuel's life unfolds. When Elkanah would divide his portion of meat between his wives and children for the sacrifice, he always gave Hannah a double portion. He did this "because he loved her, and the LORD had closed her womb" (1 Samuel 1:5).

Penninah's jealousy of the extra attention Elkanah gave to Hannah was more than she could handle. She taunted and ridiculed Hannah year after year. Domestic disputes in polygamist houses were not uncommon. It was a frequent occurrence, especially when the husband showed superior affection to the other wife, for example, Sarah and Hagar or Rachel and Leah. God's intention for marriage was always monogamous. Jesus referenced God's will in Matthew 19:4–6. God created a wife for Adam, and the two of them were to become one. A variant to the will of God will not lead to victorious living.

Elkanah tried to use words of comfort to encourage his wife: "Hannah, why are you weeping? Why don't you eat? Why are you downhearted? Don't I mean more to you than ten sons?" (v 8). Unfortunately, the answer to his question was *no*. Hannah loved her husband, yet something inside of her desired more; she wanted a family. There are no substitutes for some yearnings of the heart. You may find a salve that will ease the pain for a moment, but the longing is still there.

What happens when we continue day after day, year after year holding on to hope that comes to nothing? Maybe just when you think it is about to happen, it does not. When a false start happens several times, it can make you sick at heart. "Hope deferred makes the heart sick, but a longing fulfilled is like a tree of life" (Proverbs 13:12). Here is when we must be diligent in our prayer and devotional life and embrace God's love to fill that emptiness.

My sister, it is during these times of waiting and living with disappointment that one can easily be led into sin. If not careful, our lives will become consumed by this longing, and we can lose our way. Don't compromise your witness. Someone is watching how you live through your heartache. Focus on self-care more than ever. We become vulnerable to depression, anxiety, and even physical sickness. Stay alert, on guard that you do not become spiritually weak and susceptible to the enemy's devices. "Watch and pray that you will not fall into temptation. The spirit is willing, but the flesh is weak" (Matthew 26:41).

I have seen too many women settle for less-than trying to fill the void: less than what brings satisfaction, less than the standards previously acceptable in your life, less than what you know will produce a good outcome. If not careful, we can begin to engage in relationships that are not spiritually healthy and bring temporary satisfaction. We begin to do things and go places that previously would not have been attractive.

Stand up, my sister! Stand on the Word of God and what you already know. Get up, change positions, and change your thinking. Whatever the longings are, they should not define you! Whatever that desire may be, it doesn't take away from who or what you already have. God has designed, defined, and distinguished who you are. You are:

- chosen, holy, and blameless before God.
- a daughter of the King.
- a chosen generation, royalty.
- the apple of God's eye.
- made complete.
- God's workmanship.

Whatever you long for cannot overshadow who you already are in Christ.

Hannah arose on that morning with a new sense of purpose. She expected the same routine. Her dear husband would do his best to console her, and Peninnah would be on the sidelines to taunt and try to humiliate her. In past years, Hannah had ignored her; however, this year the taunts were the fuel that ignited something on the inside of Hannah. Hannah spoke to the One who could make a difference in the situation. She prayed to God. Her prayer was not selfish. Hannah prayed for a son, vowing that she would give this child back to God. She would give back to God her best gift: "LORD Almighty, if you will only look on your servant's misery and remember me, and not forget your servant but give her a son, then I will give him to the LORD for all the days of his life, and no razor will ever be used on his head" (1 Samuel 1:11).

Hannah's prayer was sincere as she wept loudly in the temple—so much so that she drew the attention of Eli, the priest. Eli accused her of being drunk. Even as Hannah was being disparaged, she was respectful yet firm. She did not respond negatively to Eli, but as one on a mission who refused to be distracted or denied her petition before God. " 'Not so, my lord,' Hannah replied, 'I am a woman who is deeply troubled. I have not been drinking wine or beer; I was pouring out my soul to the LORD.... I have been praying here out of my great anguish and grief' "(vv 15–16). This passionate statement represents many women down through the ages, those who would not be denied: the woman with the issue of blood who pressed her way to Jesus, the woman who anointed Jesus and would not stop her service to him, the mother who brought her demon-possessed daughter to Jesus determined that he would heal her, and he did. It is those sincere prayers that reach the heart of God.

Hannah's desire for a child was God's desire for Hannah. It was his will. "Early the next morning they arose and worshiped before the LORD and then went back to their home at Ramah. Elkanah made love to his wife

Hannah, and the Lord remembered her" (v 19). It may have taken much longer than what she or her husband wanted, but in due time, it came to pass; in the process of time, God did it. Ecclesiastes 3:1 says, "There is a time for everything, and a season for every activity under the heavens." Hannah's time to conceive did not happen until it was supposed to occur. Our due season denotes the appointed time. It is God's divine calendar, not ours. When the time is right for our prayers to be answered, God will answer them.

Maybe God is waiting for you to be ready to handle this blessing, manage it well, and not lose sight of the gift giver. There are occasions when we are not ready for what we are asking God. He uses this time to prepare us, build character, and mature and ready those who will be impacted by this answered prayer. God is not being mean or withholding anything from us. He is simply putting things in order.

Hannah's time came, and she received that which was already hers. She named her son Samuel, "Because I asked the Lord for him" (v 20). Her vow to God aligned with God's will to "in all [our] ways submit to him" (Proverbs 3:6). She gave back to God what he had given to her. Do our longings align with what God desires for us, or are they something that would bring *us* glory and attention? We must learn to give readily to the Lord. Hannah offered back to God the very thing she was asking him for. How can what we seek after bring glory back to God?

Hannah said, "After the boy is weaned, I will take him and present him before the Lord, and he will live there always" (v 22). She was true to her word. When Elkanah went to the temple to offer sacrifice the next year, Hannah did not go. Her next journey to the temple was when Samuel was weaned, and she presented him to the Lord. "As surely as you live, I am the woman who stood here beside you praying to the Lord. I prayed for this child, and…now I give him to the Lord. For his whole life he will be given over to the Lord" (vv 26–27).

Hannah used this time to prepare Samuel for his future. She poured into his life. She invested time. She did not worry about societal duties. Her family came first. She took the opportunity to help mold Samuel for his life's work. Who's shaping the minds of our children? Have we allowed all these external influences such as Xbox, social media, Netflix, or peers to replace what God intended for us to do? Hannah said, "After he is weaned...." Whatever we have longed for, desired with our whole being, we have the responsibility to be good stewards of what we asked for once we have received it.

Mothers, aunts, sisters, grandmothers, guardians, those who have taken on the role to mother our children, please do not let the enemy tell you that you cannot speak a prophecy over your children. Hannah was a true example by declaring who Samuel would be before he was born. Maybe you did not birth the child entrusted to your care, and that's okay. You still have the power to speak life, and not death, over your charge.

"Do not let any unwholesome talk come out of your mouths, but only what is helpful for building others up" (Ephesians 4:29). Words have power and must be used to build up, not tear down. Hannah declared Samuel's future before he was born. Along with this declaration was her taking responsibility for what she had the ability to do. She dedicated him as a Nazarite: "For his whole life he will be given over to the LORD" (v 28). Sure enough, Samuel lived his life in God's service.

We are in a battle for the identity of our children. Give them the foundation of truth necessary for them to overcome the temptations coming at them every day—war for your children, at any age. If you did not begin this practice at their birth, it is not too late today. Everyone needs to know that someone believes in the best they can be. Romans 4:17 says, "God...calls into being things that were not." Hannah spoke Samuel's future into existence. Beginning today, speak a blessing of hope and faith over your family. I personally began this blessing with my grandchildren: *You have been set apart to serve God, to love and worship him. Obey God's Word and keep his commandments, and you will have good success.*

Mary's song and Hannah's prayer are similar. These were two mothers whose pregnancies aligned with God's will. They both gave God praise for helping his people in their time of desperation. Hannah's prayer contained prophetic and messianic messages. She celebrated the holiness and dominion of God. Her prayer was a testament to God's intervention in her life. Many scholars remark that these passages carry a foreshadowing of God's activity in the life not only of Samuel but also those of David and the nation of Israel.

The twist and turns of Hannah's life aligned with the meaning of her name. At the beginning it was difficult to find favor, although we know grace is always present as long as we have breath in our bodies. We are never without God's grace; the challenge is how we extend that grace to others. Hannah was a gracious wife, mother, and counterpart to Peninnah. In her pain, she never stepped out of character or showed ill will toward those who ridiculed her or misunderstood her actions.

Favor, as defined by humans, is an act of kindness beyond what is due. Elkanah was kind to Hannah in this story. On the surface he appeared to be the only one who was willing to go the extra mile for Hannah. However, God's favor was ever-present. God chose Hannah, favored her to be his instrument, to shoulder this burden and model what true perseverance can accomplish.

Don't miss the gift of God's favor and grace because it is not packaged the way you imagined or hoped for. God's grace has kept us, and his favor has shown all around us.

Reflection

Often those who appear to have had a favored life are those who have also known great pain. My friend, the late Rev. Dr. Diana L. Swoope, often asked those who desired her anointing if they were equally willing to shoulder the burdens she carried.

Over 6 million women in the United States are affected by infertility. Chances are you either have experienced infertility yourself or know someone who has. This suffering has been going on since God created us. For over forty years, I bore this affliction.

I went through nine years of fertility treatments. I remember the day we found out we were pregnant. We were overjoyed. We called every family member and friend to share the wonderful news. I bless God for my brother, Dr. Wes, who shared my joy, yet cautiously added that we needed to go through further testing to make certain this could be a viable pregnancy. I heeded his words yet continued for several weeks in a state of euphoria.

And then there came the day when things changed. On that day, I lost the child we had hoped for and my ability to have children. Hope deferred became hope lost. This has been the thorn that I carried, one that I prayed for many years to be removed. For some time, I lost sight of God's grace and surely did not feel favored. I was angry, hurt, disappointed, and distraught. Then I heard a message preached on the Shunammite woman who lost her son. Upon her son's death, her response was, "It is well" (2 Kings 4:26, KJV). God's love and the prompting of his Spirit penetrated the depths of my despair and healed me.

God's answer to my prayer for a child did not end the way I had expected. Even today I have no answers as to why, but *it is well with my soul.* I have learned to live with joy and with sadness. Both come unexpectedly, out of our control. Yet, one thing I am sure of during pain and prosperity, joy and despair is a truth I have framed and placed in my office: I *expect the favor of God every day*. His favor may appear to be disguised in trials and tests, but it produces an undeniable testimony.

I share this story because I have silently watched the pain in the eyes of the women who sit in our circles, share a meal with the crowd, and attend our meetings. Without them saying it, I see their faces, their pain, and sometimes their shame. I have watched them and quietly prayed for them. I can see in their eyes that their stories are like mine. If the telling of my story will help another woman on her road to wholeness, then it is worth it.

Hannah's affliction was not a new ailment. From the story, we can see she had been living with this condition for many years. All the while, Peninnah had one child after another. Silently, Hannah kept going to the temple and hearing a word from God. Did the teachings apply to her? Where were her blessings? Where was the fruit of her womb? What had her pious living brought her? It brought her hope. She took her hope to the One in control. Hannah *petitioned* God. She ran to God. She knew to run to the only one who could help. She did not allow her emotions to overtake her faith. Emotions will cause us to react; El Shaddai, God Almighty, will call us to action. He will call us to the throne of grace, where we receive mercy.

It is hard today for people to hear a message of hope. So many are walking around feeling hopeless and helpless. My sister, this must not be you and me. Hope in Christ is our anchor, our stabilizer. An anchor provides stability and safety in dangerous waters. It holds the ship in place, keeps it from drifting. No matter the trial or test facing you today, don't drift or wander away from what you know is true.

The Message Bible has a wonderful translation for Hebrews 6:18–20:

> When God wanted to guarantee his promises, he gave his word, a rock-solid guarantee—God *can't* break his word. And because his word cannot change, the promise is likewise unchangeable. We who have run for our very lives to God have every reason to grab the promised hope with both hands and never let go. It's an unbreakable spiritual lifeline, reaching past all appearances right to the very presence of God where Jesus, running on ahead of us, has taken up his permanent post as high priest for us.

Paul was writing this letter to the people of God, those who had tasted the Holy Spirit and knew the power of God. He admonished them: don't lose heart. We who proclaim ourselves Christ-followers must hold on to our faith, even during challenging times. When prayers seem to go unanswered, don't lose hope. Hope is our anchor; it is the confidence we have in God that we are his children through Christ Jesus.

This concept is hard for a non-believer to grasp. David described it this way, "Some trust in chariots and some in horses, but we trust in the name of the LORD" (Psalm 20:7). Call on the one who, when he speaks, it is established, accomplished—past tense. There are times when we mistakenly believe we have the power to solve our problems. Or maybe we feel that this is happening to us because God is mad at us because of something awful we did. God's ways are not like that; he is simply inviting us to call on him.

Our hope in Christ is also the belief that things will improve or change, as Hannah believed. God honored Hannah's faith. When she departed the temple, she was no longer downcast; she ate and believed her prayer would be answered. She began to take care of herself in preparation for conceiving this child.

When we put our faith in him, God enters our *process*. Our life is in God's hands, and he will bring us through to a place where we can see all the ways his hand was guiding us. A calm suddenly washed over this story of desperation. There was no longer the spirit of anxiousness and anxiety but peace and reassurance.

Hannah's waiting now was filled with hope and expectancy. The waiting room is a part of everyone's life. We can spend that time complaining and fretting or use the time for worship and growth. "Those who hope in the LORD will renew their strength" (Isaiah 40:31). Waiting and hope are often used interchangeably in the Scriptures. When we wait, filled with hope, it suggests something is yet to come.

God is continually speaking to us as we go through tough situations. If we are sensitive to his promptings, he will guide our steps. He desires for us to have those hard conversations with him. He already knows how you feel about his decision regarding your situation. He is waiting; Scripture says, "You will…find me when you seek me with all your heart" (Jeremiah 29:13).

What are you doing while waiting? Are you busy or bemoaning? The rest of the scripture in Isaiah 40:31 says, "soar…run…walk and not be faint." Don't let the enemy defeat you any longer while waiting; God has heard the longings of your heart.

God hears our petitions; he enters our process of waiting in *preparation* for the fulfillment of his promise. Our hope in Christ is our certainty that God is faithful and he hears us. Hannah's prayer was for a son that she would give back to God. What she did not know was the impact this child would have on a nation. She was offering his service to the priest, yet God had something greater. Samuel became a notable figure in Israel's history. He would play a pivotal role in the transition from judges to kings; Samuel anointed the first two kings of Israel.

What happens when God improves on what you have asked him for? There are wonderful things bound up in our letdowns. God will not allow our brokenness to be the final word. His answer may be different from what we imagined, but rest assured, it is always for our good. During these times, he is building character and perseverance. Our disappointments bring God's desired blessings. When we look back, we see that every door that was closed was an opportunity for a new door to open.

Our prayer had been for a child. Within a three-year span, God blessed us with four children. I was relatively young but old enough that the thought of having three children was out of the question. God gave us his best.

I love movies with tension and life lessons. One of my favorite movies is about a woman who lost a child when she was younger; she had given up on the idea of having more children. Then she meets this baby and chooses to raise this child despite her life circumstances and past hurts. There is a tender moment of this mother and son having a conversation. She shares the pain of losing that child and then looks at her son with the love of a mother and says, "I was angry with God for a long time, but then he gave me you." My children know this movie and this scene well. Every time it is on, if they are in the house, I call them into the room and remind them of being the best gift in my life. God answered my prayers differently than expected, but he also exceeded all expectations.

Hannah's prayer was one of thanksgiving for God's sovereignty: his knowing what was best. She was grateful for the favor given to her and access to his grace. God fulfilled his promise, and so did Hannah.

Conclusion

Where are you right now? Do you have a petition before God? Trust that he hears you. Maybe it's been a long time coming, but don't lose hope. God is at work in this process. Look for him. Did he answer the prayer differently from how you expected? Praise him for the perfect answer. You desired good, and God has given you great.

Questions for Reflection

1. "There are no substitutes to some yearnings of the heart." Reflect on the top three yearnings of your heart. In what ways have you tried or are you trying to fill those yearnings? Do these ways glorify God?

2. What is most important to you in your life right now? In what ways could you give that as a "gift" to God?

3. Describe a time you had a petition or prayer before God that took a long time for an answer due to the fact that you had to be prepared for that answer.

4. Have you experienced a "false start" due to a prayer being answered that didn't work out? If so, how did your hope remain steadfast?

CHAPTER 9

God Knows Us!

He knows us far better than we know ourselves, knows our pregnant condition, and keeps us present before God. That's why we can be so sure that every detail in our lives of love for God is worked into something good. God knew what he was doing from the very beginning. He decided from the outset to shape the lives of those who love him along the same lines as the life of his Son. —Romans 8:27–29, MSG

There are times when it seems life takes a sudden turn. Perhaps it's problems with our health, relationships, difficulties at work, or a tragedy in our family. It is during those times we must be careful that we do not spiral downward while seeking answers. God is in control of our lives. Answers may not be readily available, but remain faithful. God may be using this sudden turn to shape your future and to reach others.

This passage of Scripture is the assurance that God knows us better than we know ourselves. He is aware of every detail of our lives. He knows our feelings, actions, preferences, desires, and dreams. We can't hide from him; he knows us, and we cannot shock him by our actions.

We live in a world driven by appearances, the desire to be successful, and too often looking for fame rather than substance. When things happen unexpectedly to us that take us off our projected course, how do we respond? Do we become desperate to recover what was lost, or do we trust God for direction?

The life of Anna speaks volumes about one who clearly was not living the life she had planned in her younger years. After experiencing great loss, she turned wholeheartedly to God. She chose to see this as an opportunity to serve God more and found great fulfillment in her choice.

Anna: A Life Fulfilled

Luke 2:36–38

After almost four hundred years of silence, Anna was the first person recorded in the New Testament as a prophet. Her life bore witness to Christ and her unmovable faith in the coming Messiah. She lived with wholeness because she held on to her faith. If the length of one's bio or vita is the litmus test for success, Anna would have missed the mark. She did not have books named for her, chapters written in her honor, or cities that identified her origin of birth. She had two sentences included in Mary and Joseph's narrative presenting Jesus at the temple for the first time. Although quite brief, we know who she was, the character and substance of this woman. Even in this small description of their meeting, we hear of the tragedy in her life, but we are left with her significance.

Anna lived during ancient times when Jewish customs severely constrained the status and freedoms of women. They were considered inferior to men and under their authority. Anna was the daughter of Phanuel, and her father was from the tribe of Asher. Asher was one of the northern tribes lost during exile. Anna was probably not viewed as a person of influence and may have been overlooked. But when others cannot see you or underestimate your value, God knows your name.

Anna was a widow, advanced in age, whose husband died after seven years of marriage. There is no record of her husband's name or lineage. After his death, she remained a widow for eighty-four years. As a widow living within the boundaries of Jewish customs, she was without a covering. She could have looked upon herself with self-pity. She could have bemoaned her future; instead, she devoted her life to worship and service in the temple. A fulfilled life is not based on your circumstances, bank account, notoriety, or human rubrics of success; it is built on Christ within us, our hope of glory.

Luke records that after the death of Anna's husband, "She never left the temple but worshiped night and day, fasting and praying" (2:37). His description of her lifestyle may seem eccentric to us today, as was probably the case at that time also. Anna found her purpose, the thing that invigorated her and gave her a reason each day to rise. She found a place to belong and serve faithfully. She never left her post unattended. Theologians question whether Anna lived in the temple, for there was no place for habitation; whatever the case, maybe she spent most of her waking hours there committed to her calling.

Anna could have chosen to live a depressing life, solitary and alone. But she chose to be in an atmosphere where she was needed. Her husband may have died, but her hope did not. She may have lost her earthly love, but God gave her more of himself, and Anna thrived in this relationship. For eighty-five years, she served. Bitterness had no place in Anna's world; she lived each day overflowing with anticipation.

Nothing is haphazard with God; whatever we are going through, God already knows. He knows the loss, the detours, and the unexpected turn of events in your life. Whatever we may need, God has already provided for it. Ephesians 2:10 says, "We are God's handiwork, created in Christ Jesus to do good works, which God prepared in advance for us to do." My sister, find comfort in this verse. God already knows! He knows, and he has already ordained your success and good works. The setbacks or slip-ups, the problems or possibilities—the loss is the latter rain.

Anna did not take a corner seat or back seat delegated for the women only; she joined openly in prayer. She modeled self-control and discipline in her fasting as well. Choosing to abide in the temple early on was a decision that meant she was able to crucify the flesh. I can imagine her depth of understanding and the sacrifices she was willing to make to conquer the lifestyle she chose.

We will never be able to achieve a more stable lifestyle unless we are willing to surrender something. Anna seemed to understand that a life of power was a commitment on her part to live a disciplined life. When the disciples questioned Jesus as to why they could not drive out the evil spirit, Jesus responded to them, "This kind can come out only by prayer" (Mark 9:29). In other words, there are things we face in life that we cannot accomplish without extra power from God. Anna understood that her worship was important, but her power came from seeking a stronger relationship with God.

"Coming up to them at that very moment" (Luke 2:38)—this was the moment Anna had been waiting for. She had listened to the reading of the scrolls and sacred Scriptures. She believed in the prophecies concerning the coming of the Messiah. It was no coincidence that Anna was there, in the temple as Simeon was proclaiming, "For my eyes have seen your salvation" (Luke 2:30). I am sure it was hard for her to contain her joy. All of the years invested and hours spent in prayer brought great rewards. Her faithfulness brought her into the presence of God, not just spiritually, but she could touch, see, and feel his presence.

Moments such as this are not reserved only for Anna; God has something in store for each one of us who are willing to do the work and do our part to receive the power of God in our lives. We, too, will reap the rewards and behold his goodness in tangible ways.

Don't give up or give in to the enemy who speaks defeat. Even in the worst of circumstances, God is with us. Anna refused to be defined by her station in life. She was more than an aging widow; she was who God said she would be. When life does not go as expected, you can still hold on to the truth that God is sovereign; he knows your name and has your future in his sight.

Anna praised God for his faithfulness not only to her but also to her people: "She gave thanks to God and spoke about the child to all who were looking forward to the redemption of Jerusalem" (v 38). She became a witness to what she had seen and heard. Anna, the prophetess, received insight and recognized who Jesus was. She gladly shared with others her hope and her faith.

Anna's life became a testimony of suffering and salvation. God used her to reach out to others. Age, economic status, education, and ethnicity are qualifiers for what God has for each one of us to do. All the details that make you who you are—these are the exact components necessary to accomplish the task. Anna was an aging widow, living in a male-dominated society, and she became the first female herald of the incarnation to all who were looking for the Redeemer.

Anna's truth, what she held on to, is our truth today. God doesn't change! Our circumstances and feelings may shift, but he changes not. We can be assured that in every detail of our lives, the love of God is at work to bring about good. It is not in vain.

Reflection

Each of us can remember a time when suddenly what we thought would be significant and lasting in our lives came to an end. It was our time in the valley. The valley is hard, unwanted, and wearing on our mind, body, and soul. It zaps us of our energy, and if we are not careful, it will steal our identity. While in the valley, we look for answers and hopefully a way out. Anna's life is an example of endurance during trying times. Prayer and fasting need to be routine—not a go-to fix, but a lifestyle. Anna gained the strength to live through and was not consumed and overwhelmed by her circumstances. What are we willing to give up to live victoriously?

Don't let the devices of the enemy trick you into believing that God doesn't care, that he is painfully silent. God is not silent. The events of our lives are not chance or meaningless. They are divinely placed there for a reason. God desires for us to be more like Christ and dependent upon him rather than living with false security in others or other things. God will sometimes remove things and people from our lives to draw our attention back to him. Living a fulfilled life happens when our dependency is on God alone as the supplier of our needs.

Paul understood what it was to live a fulfilled life: "I have learned to be content whatever the circumstances. I know what it is to be in need, and I know what it is to have plenty. I have learned the secret of being content in any and every situation, whether well fed or hungry, whether living in plenty or in want. I can do all this through him who gives me strength" (Philippians 4:11–13).

We can glean this principle from Anna's life: Don't focus so much on the cracks in the track; focus more on the race and the desire to finish well.

Hundreds of thousands of memories woven together make up a life. Every one of us can remember that *defining memory*: the occurrence that changed the course of our life. It memorialized an event and became pivotal in how you responded to life's unfortunate and often untimely episodes.

Isaiah wrote, "In the year that King Uzziah died, I saw the Lord" (6:1). The prophet Isaiah traced the memory that would define his ministry; it was the year of the king's death. When Luke told Anna's story, he marked a memory, "She was very old; she had lived with her husband seven years after marriage, and then was a widow until she was eighty-four" (Luke 2:36–37). Anna's life changed. Her dream of being a wife and a mother was gone. That memory was housed between a few details concerning her origin and what she did after her husband's death.

The poem *The Dash* illustrates the importance of the "dash" that separates the date of a person's birth and the date of her or his passing. Unfortunately, there are too many people who die inside as the result of a memory. They stop believing, hoping, and desiring a better way. Memories can bind us and restrict positive motion, or they can propel us into a new way of living.

There must have been something inside of Anna that chose life. Luke may not have articulated it, but her actions showed her courage and will to survive. In a culture where women were not equal to men, even in the temple, Anna seemed to excel. She was a full participant in life. Anna was not defined by the loss of her husband. Her identity was more than just the wife of an unknown man. She was a prophetess, one who proclaims a divine message. She chose to live her dash to the fullest.

It is hard to let go of some memories; we rehearse them over and over. Unfortunately, this behavior means we keep reliving the sadness and despair as well. Eventually, we must ask ourselves, "Do I want to live an abundant life? Do I want to live free?" Trials and heartache have their usefulness. We must learn to place them in their proper category for our testing and our growth. Don't waste your grief; shift the way you think and respond. Use those times to gain strength for the next season of difficulty. When we build up resistant muscles to discouragement and despair, the next set of tests will be easier to conquer. However, this only occurs when we decide to live victoriously and not as victims.

Maybe facing your sorrow includes forgiveness or letting go of past hurts. The process of healing involves uprooting bad behaviors. Forgiveness requires work; it means letting go and not allowing yourself to be locked in the past. There are so many memories that can hold us back and lock us in sorrow. We can make excuse after excuse for why we are not living life to its fullest, but it's up to us. "When Jesus saw him lying there and *learned that he had been in this condition for a long time*, he asked him, 'Do you want to get well?' " (John 5:6, emphasis added). Anna did not allow her memory to become a hindrance, but she allowed it to be helpful to steady her for the future.

At that very moment became significant in Anna's life. This was a *defining* moment for Anna. A defining moment is transformative. It is when you experience something that fundamentally changes you and how you view life. Here are some examples:

For Rahab—hiding the spies who would later save her family.

For the Samaritan woman—meeting Jesus at the well.

For Ruth—deciding to follow Naomi.

For the widow of Zarephath—meeting Elijah.

For Lydia—meeting Paul at the riverside.

Each of these women experienced something beyond their human experience. God moved them away from their personal paradigm. As a result, their lives were never the same.

I remember a defining moment in my life. I was having a conversation with my sister-in-law. She was counseling me through a difficult season of my life. She said, "Netta, you need a plan." I had to admit what she said to me had never occurred to me before. I was unprepared for what was happening in my life. While the event was devastating, it was not a sudden action. However, it was a new paradigm and much different from how I had perceived my future. I had to make new commitments and engage in new disciplines.

I did not have a plan *B* or *C*. I had only accounted for plan *A*.

As I look back now, the decision I made during that season of my life changed my trajectory. More importantly than what I did, it was what I allowed God to do. I recognized that I truly had no control, and I yielded to the way of God unconditionally. There was no place or no one I could depend on with certainty, other than God. He showed himself mighty in one of the darkest periods of my life. That brief conversation sent me to the throne of God.

Defining moments bring clarity and take us to a new dimension. They are often moments of refreshing and renewal. For Christians, one of those moments should be the day of our salvation, the day we met Jesus face-to-face. He no longer was just the Savior of our parents, Sunday school teacher, or friend. He became personal to us. Don't miss your moment, your God moment. There's more than one moment if you keep your heart and mind open to receive. These moments will lead you down a path that God ordained from the foundation of the world.

Anna could have allowed her worst moments to define her life, but she chose what she knew of the coming Messiah and her encounter with

Jesus instead to have a greater impact. Anna's life was forever changed because of Jesus. For many years she had worshipped inside of the temple. Immediately after she saw him, even as a baby, her witness expanded beyond the walls of the temple.

Anna's defining moment led to her *defining* message. The strength of life's defining message will unveil the ambiguities of how God uses your ordinary to do the extraordinary. Your everyday experiences have formed you into the unique creation you are. Your message will ring loud and clear as you walk with confidence into the person God created you to be.

For my readers over forty, you can relate to the following analogy. For those younger, I will do my best to explain. Once upon a time, we had what was called redeemable bottles. We would wait for our parents, grandparents, and neighbors to consume their soft drinks to take the empty bottle to the store for $.05. In the 1960s, a nickel would buy enough candy for you and your friends. Anna believed in the Messiah, the one coming to bring redemption to the world. She lived her life year after year, anticipating his coming. She lived knowing that Jesus was coming to redeem those empties, the empty places that had overtaken the hearts, minds, and souls of his people, and fill them with the overflow of his love.

Conclusion

May your defining message speak with authority:

- I am who God says I am.
- I am no longer broken but made whole in Christ.
- I am fearfully and wonderfully made.
- I am more than a conqueror.
- I am chosen and set apart for service.
- I am the one to bear witness to the saving power of Jesus.
- I am heir to the Kingdom, co-heir with Christ.

Our message to the world is simple: hardship, handicaps, setbacks, persecution, and failures will not define us. We are children of the Most High God; we are treasured, loved, and valued beyond measure and will walk therein.

Questions for Reflection

1. Have you ever had an experience of losing something that left you feeling hopeless? In what ways did you experience God giving more of himself to you?

2. Reflect on a time in your life when you needed the extra power of God. What did you do differently to seek this power—for example, worship, prayer, yielding, counsel, or something else?

3. "Defining moments bring clarity." Think of a moment in your life that was a catalyst for a new dimension, season, or level of renewal. Was that moment painful or joyful? How long did it take you to fully embrace the painful moment or experience a joyful clarity?

PART 4

God's Placement

CHAPTER 10

Generational Impact

"I will establish my covenant as an everlasting covenant between me and you and your descendants after you for the generations to come, to be your God and the God of your descendants after you."
—Genesis 17:7

God forms covenants with families; he honors his word if we do our part. Abraham had to follow the commands of God to unleash God's blessings to his family. How often have you witnessed generations of believers because it began generations before? The Bible is filled with examples of faith being passed to the next generation, so that they may know the wonders God has done.

Sharing Christ with your family is setting them up to succeed. When you expose the next generation to God you are aiding your family in preparation for their future. Joshua made a decision for his family: "If serving the Lord seems undesirable to you, then choose for yourselves this day whom you will serve.... But as for me and my household, we will serve the Lord" (Joshua 24:15). Our families are disposed to make their own choices, but they will remember the choices you made before them.

Some people are blessed to have been introduced early to God. Rahab provided this gift to her family, yet she was not fortunate to have received the same beginning. This is proof that God's grace is available to everyone.

Generational impact is akin to helping your family make wise financial decisions. Introducing them to financial advisors early on helps them make wise investments, which allows for a more prosperous future. Sharing Christ is one of the greatest investments you can make in the lives of your children and grandchildren. "One generation commends your works to another; they tell of your mighty acts" (Psalm 145:4).

Impacting the next generation is ensuring that our actions align with our words. "I am reminded of your sincere faith, which first lived in your grandmother Lois and in your mother Eunice and, I am persuaded, now lives in you also" (2 Timothy 1:5). Live your faith before your children. Your faith may not be perfect, but it has great bearing on your life every day.

Rahab: Family Impact

Joshua 2:1–22; 6:17–25

Even today, you can find conflicting thoughts regarding Rahab's profession. Josephus records her as being an innkeeper. However, the Greek word *porne* is used when she is mentioned in Hebrews 11:31 and James 2:25; *porne* clearly means harlot/prostitute. Those who support her being an innkeeper also believe she became the wife of Joshua. Accepting the definition of harlot in the New Testament aligns with Matthew 1:5 and her inclusion in the genealogy of Jesus. [9]

Rahab grew up in the pagan city of Jericho. She was an industrious woman who is believed to have had the ability to weave fine linen from the dried flax she kept at her home. She is celebrated for being one of two women mentioned in the Hebrews "hall of faith." Her life is a true example that your beginning does not define your ending. Rahab carried the banner for the remainder of her life as being a woman with extraordinary faith. She, like the apostle Paul, was chosen by God to play a key role in his redemptive story.

We know that Rahab had family, parents, and siblings at the time of her alliance with the spies, but there is no listing of their names. She was the wife of Salmon and the mother of Boaz, who married Ruth. Some scholars say her husband was a prince of the house of Judah, which means she married into one of the leading families of Israel.

Before launching his attack, Joshua sent out spies telling them to survey the land, especially Jericho. This city was key in Joshua's advancement to enter Palestine from the east. "Joshua son of Nun secretly sent two spies from Shittim. 'Go, look over the land,' he said, 'especially Jericho.' So they went and entered the house of a prostitute named Rahab and stayed there" (Joshua 2:1). Rahab's home was in a key position built over the gap between the two walls of the city. Because of her frequent visitors, one might imagine this would be a great place to go unnoticed. Choosing her house might have served as an inconspicuous location, but someone leaked the word to the king that they were there.

The king of Jericho sent word to Rahab, "Bring out the men who came to you and entered your house" (Joshua 2:3). Here is where Rahab was

9 William Whiston, *The Works of Josephus* (Peabody, MA: Hendrickson Publishers, 1987), 126.

faced with a major decision. She was aware of the great exploits God had performed on behalf of the Israelites. She knew of how he had parted the Red Sea and of the overthrow of Sihon and Og. If she disobeyed and was caught, she could be killed for treason. At that moment, she had to make a decision. She lied: "Yes, the men came to me, but I did not know where they had come from. At dusk, when it was time to close the city gate, they left. I don't know which way they went" (Joshua 2:4–5).

Each one of us has faced crossroads in our lives. We have had to make a decision quickly regarding our future and the well-being of our families. What influences such a decision? Is it anxiousness, or is our decision grounded in what we know about God? Rahab referenced what she knew of God's track record to bring relief to her and her family: "I know that the Lord has given you this land and that a great fear of you has fallen on us, so that all who live in this country are melting in fear because of you" (Joshua 2:9).

Rahab hid the spies on the roof in the flax stalks. As she ascended the stairs to where they had been hiding, she must have had thoughts of her life and her family. She also recognized that she was making a life choice. She was ready to give up everything she had known and valued. Rahab was making a turn away from idolatry and toward Jehovah in hopes for a better life. She also had a deep concern for the salvation of her family: "Now then, please swear to me by the Lord that you will show kindness to my family, because I have shown kindness to you. Give me a sure sign that you will spare the lives of my father and mother, my brothers and sisters, and all who belong to them—and that you will save us from death" (Joshua 2:12–13).

Divine connections are tools in God's economy. Only he could orchestrate the spies going to the house of the one person who would be sensitive to their assignment. Surely, God was already working in the heart of Rahab to receive them and offer safety at the expense of her own life. The spies saw her desire for change, exemplifying the heart of God. They agreed to what she proposed: " 'Our lives for your lives!' the men assured her. 'If you don't tell what we are doing, we will treat you kindly and faithfully when the Lord gives us the land' " (Joshua 2:14).

Jericho was one of the worst cities in the Amorite nation. God had commanded Joshua to bring about the total destruction of all its inhabitants. When we are willing to intervene and pray on behalf of our family, we never know the dangers that may have been thwarted as a result of our prayers.

Kelly Coeland Kutz says in her book *Protecting Your Family in Dangerous Times*, "It's easy to say, Oh, I do believe that God will protect my family from harm. But we must be sure of the fact and respond in faith. Our access into God's grace is by faith. You have to aggressively lay hold to your right because the Word says it is true."[10]

Jericho was in danger; Rahab acknowledged that the whole city was *melting in fear* at the thought of being attacked. Yet, this woman believed she was already operating from the place of a covenant with God. She aggressively laid hold to her faith that if she assisted the people of God, her family would be spared.

My sister, we have the power and the authority to come boldly to the throne of grace on behalf of our families. Are we willing to be radical for the sake of saving our loved ones? Are we ready to save our children from the pressures they face when we are not present? Will we save our marriages from the enemy of repetition and competition? How often do we use the words of Isaiah with undeniable faith, " 'No weapon forged against you will prevail, and you will refute every tongue that accuses you. This is the heritage of the servants of the Lord, and this is their vindication from me,' declares the Lord" (Isaiah 54:17)?

Continuing to exercise her faith, Rahab offered advice to the spies for their escape. She lowered them down by a heavy rope probably woven from the flax stalks on her roof. The men made an oath with Rahab for when they returned. Destruction and death would not enter her home if she tied a scarlet cord on her window. However, it was up to Rahab to gather all her family members under her roof for protection.

There is so much that can be said for what the spies asked of Rahab. Many commentaries talk about the scarlet cord representing the Passover. Moses had instructed the people to mark their doors with lamb's blood, which would be a sign, and the angel of death would pass over and all the inhabitants would be safe. How interesting that the cord Rahab used just happened to be red.

---

10 Kelly Coeland Kutz, *Protecting Your Family in Dangerous Times* (Tulsa, OK: Harrison House, Inc., 2002), 79–80.

The spies also instructed Rahab to display a unified existence with her family. They did not limit who or how many. They mentioned mother, father, and brothers, but then they said, "and all your family" (v 18). Being a unified family will have a greater witness than all the church services you may ever attend. God dwells in our unity: "How good and how pleasant it is when God's people live together in unity.... For there the LORD bestows his blessing" (Psalm 133:1, 3). The Christian life is undesirable to the world when they see damaged relations, broken marriages, and infighting. As a family, we must seek to be of one mind and heart. Living in harmony with one another sets God's people apart from the world. For Rahab and her family, all who wanted to be saved, to be spared from the attack, had to choose unity and to live in harmony with those who worshipped God.

When the spies returned and brought their report back to Joshua, they also told him of their encounter with Rahab.

Joshua would remember the promise made to Rahab and her family and would honor it. "The seventh time around, when the priests sounded the trumpet blast, Joshua commanded the army, 'Shout! For the LORD has given you the city! The city and all that is in it are to be devoted to the LORD. Only Rahab the prostitute and all who are with her in her house shall be spared, because she hid the spies we sent' " (Joshua 6:16–17). Joshua and his army killed everyone in the city and then burned the city to the ground; everyone perished but Rahab and her family.

When we live by faith, we can trust God to be faithful to us. Even in our imperfection, God is at work perfecting those things concerning us. Who Rahab was is not as important as who she became. This story was Rahab's journey in search of God.

Rahab's choice of profession was not that of a childhood dream. Perhaps her life choices had separated her from her family. When she proposed to the spies her conditional help, she had to bring her family to her. One can imagine there may have been a breach in relations. Even as she was providing aid to the spies, she lied to protect them. Many have questioned her method used to provide aid. It is tempting to judge since we are removed from this situation, peering at her choice through the lens of our own experiences to evaluate her actions. For Rahab, I believe she was simply doing her best to please God. Her deceit is not commended in this text but her faith, which was the driving force of her conduct.

When the battle was over, Joshua remembered Rahab: "Joshua said to the two men who had spied out the land, 'Go into the prostitute's house and bring her out and all who belong to her, in accordance with your oath to her.' So the young men who had done the spying went in and brought out Rahab, her father and mother, her brothers and sisters and all who belonged to her. They brought out her entire family and put them in a place outside the camp of Israel" (Joshua 6:22–23).

What excites me even more about this story is that it ends with the same characters with which it began. Salmon was one of the spies deployed to view the land; he was one whom she hid and protected. When Joshua sent Salmon to go get Rahab and her family, Salmon didn't know it at the time, but he was going back to get his bride.

"By faith the prostitute Rahab, because she welcomed the spies, was not killed with those who were disobedient" (Hebrews 11:31).

Reflection

Rahab was a strong woman. Putting aside for a moment her profession, she was a single woman living in a male-dominated society. She was hard-working and productive. Even as a prostitute, she also had another trade. The flax stalks and the cords provided for the spies to escape indicated that she was multifaceted. She was a woman who *persevered* against all odds. Clearly, she had tenacity and was not one to give up. When the king's men came to her house, she could have crumbled at their questioning, yet she was a quick thinker.

My sister, if Rahab could make it, so can we. We can because of the God we serve and what he has put on the inside of us to endure. All of us were put on this planet to make a difference. When we breathe our last breath, the world should be in a better place because we lived. Whatever you are up against, it is not greater than God. "You, dear children, are from God and have overcome them, because the one who is in you is greater than the one who is in the world" (1 John 4:4).

Rahab's perseverance was not for her benefit alone; she was determined for her family. There are times when we must be "warrior mothers" for our families. We must be willing at any cost to seek the preservation of our homes. There may be other influences to aid you along the way, such as teachers, coaches, and other forces in your family's life. However, no force should be greater or have more of an impact than yours.

Seek to be the voice inside of your children's heads. What do I mean? In your absence, they can still hear your godly counsel. They can hear you when they are facing pressure to make wrong decisions.

Recently I was riding with my son in his car, and he was scanning through all his music. Since my children were young, my rule has always been the driver gets to choose the music. When they were younger, it gave me control over what we listened to; now, I am captive to their preferences when I am in their car. His choices that day went from rap to rock to R&B, and then he switched to the CD already in the car. It was one of my old CDs with several artists of my liking: the Winans, Brooklyn Tabernacle, Carlton Pearson, and so forth. As this CD began to play, he sang every song, one after the other. I jokingly said to him, "How is it you know all the words to these songs?"

He looked at me out of the corner of his eye and said, "Mom, that's all we knew; that's all you let us listen to growing up." It dawned on me that while the other music was playing he never sang or rapped to the beat. Yet, when the songs of God came on, he joined in.

Why do I tell this story? Because I persevered for my children. I was dogged then, and I am that way today for them to know Christ. I have not been close to perfection, but I have been persistent. While I have been driven to share my faith, I also knew it was important for me to *show* my faith. There are times when my children's choices were not what I would have hoped, but I have never wavered in the way I speak of them to God and others. They are a chosen generation, and I know God is yet working out his will in their lives.

Rahab was a woman who was willing to *provide*; she had a real concern to help others. Serving God manifests itself so often in how we serve others. Rahab's provision was not just for her and her family, but it extended to strangers as well.

Being a person who provides for others doesn't mean you are a person with unlimited resources. However, it means that you are in relationship with the God who will make available his unlimited resources to you if you ask. If we want our children to be community-minded, it begins with us. "[Look] not only to your own interests but each of you to the interests of the others" (Philippians 2:4).

Modeling generational impact should include our willingness to share what we have with others. It is like the boy with the two fish and five loaves of bread. Place the little that you have in God's hands and watch him multiply your gift. It's having the widow's mite but giving it freely, expecting nothing in return. Your reward is in your giving. The four friends willing to burst through the roof to get their paraplegic friend to Jesus were modeling generational impact. Peter did it through his honesty when he said, "Silver or gold I do not have, but what I do have I give you. In the name of Jesus Chris of Nazareth, walk" (Acts 3:6).

Our families will watch how we live out our faith before others and give our time, talent, and resources. They will watch how we balance our first ministry to them as being of the utmost importance.

An article written by Family Life states, "I never thought learning songs, watching my parents read, or thinking about beautiful things would change my life, but they have. My day-in and day-out interactions with God would not look the same without having lived with parents who demonstrated spiritually healthy lives. I am forever grateful and hope to do the same with a family of my own one day." [11]

Rahab's selfless behavior spoke volumes to her family as well as to the spies. Being careful not to make a sweeping statement that will bring offense, we seem to be living in a time when family is no longer looking out for family. I have often been surprised at the needs of those brought to our attention and families who are not willing to assist. Yes, I know there are some dynamics we must consider; unfortunately, it is becoming the norm. Rahab's protection of her family was fierce. When she asked the spies to show kindness for her aid, she did not say for my family and me; her statement was clear. In the original language, she asked that they show kindness to her *father's household.* Yes, this request may have included her, but it certainly was not one of exclusion.

There are times when our loved ones need to know that no matter what they are going through, they will not be alone. Psalm 139:8 says, "If I go up to the heavens, you are there; if I make my bed in the depths, you are there." If God chooses to stand with us, no matter what, we as his people should do the same. Being there for loved ones in difficult times

11 Lauren Miller, "5 Ways My Parents Shaped My Spiritual Life," Family Life, accessed April 1, 2021, https://d1ueb8h0efn28g.cloudfront.net/articles/topics/parenting/foundations/spiritual-development/5-ways-my-parents-shaped-my-spiritual-life/.

can bring cohesion within the family. Showing up and being present is sometimes all the protection they need.

Conclusion

God established a relationship with Rahab and her family through a chance encounter. Her impact on her family extended for generations and is still alive today. How are you influencing your family in advancing the Kingdom?

Someone, maybe a family member, desperately wants to change her or his life. This person wants to but doesn't know how to bring Kingdom impact about. You know the struggle. You have witnessed this person's choices; she or he needs help. God is saying, "Whom are you going after?" Remember, someone came back for you. Maybe it was a parent, teacher, pastor, or friend, but someone remembered us. We were worth saving, and so are they. Go get Rahab!

Questions for Reflection

1. "Your beginning does not define your ending." Everyone has an origin story. Reflect on a redemptive story in your life from the beginning to now. What drastic change resonates with you?
2. "Each one of us have faced crossroads in our lives." Have you ever had to make a quick decision regarding not only your future, but also the future of your family, community, friends, and all who "belong to you"? Through anxiety or peace, what influenced that decision?
3. What "roles" have you had to play for your family, friends, or community? Have you been warrior, peacemaker, nurturer, coach, provider, negotiator, or something else? How has God used that role to bless others?

CHAPTER 11

Everyday Impact

"Let your light shine before others, that they may see your good deeds and glorify your Father in heaven." —*Matthew 5:16*

Be the light, wherever you are. Where you live, work, play, shop, or go for a needed respite is not by chance. That is the place for you to shine. As children of the light, we have a responsibility every day to be light-bearers.

God has entrusted our communities into our care. Throughout the Scriptures, we have seen women just like you whose light broke through the dawn despite their placement or standing. Lydia's light shone brightly as she and the women gathered for prayer. Paul expected to find a man searching for his Macedonia call, but he found a faithful band of women praying.

Deborah's light was shown as a wise judge in whom Barak had great confidence. Because she lived in a community of light-bearers, she stepped into the shadows and allowed Jael's light to shine and receive the credit.

In Titus 2, older women modeled for younger women how to shine brightly in their homes and the marketplace as women of discipline and grace.

Sister, we are called to our communities, the inner cities, and rural and suburban neighborhoods to share our message of hope, love, and unity.

"You are the light of the world. A town built on a hill cannot be hidden. Neither do people light a lamp and put it under a bowl. Instead they put it on its stand, and it gives light to everyone in the house" (Matthew 5:14–15). Let it shine, let it shine, let it shine.

Esther: Community Impact

The Book of Esther

Esther's story is unique in many ways; she is the first prominent woman in the Scripture who lived outside of Palestine. She also had the distinction of being a member of an elite club of two; she and Ruth are the only two women with books in the Bible named for them. Surely, we can classify both as being light-bearers.

Esther's Jewish name was Hadassah; in Hebrew, the word means *myrtle.* After she became queen, her name was changed to Esther, and in Hebrew, this means *star.* Esther was born in Susa, which was absorbed by Persia after the exile.

Esther is introduced as an orphan and cousin to Mordecai, a Benjamite, who had been taken captive during the reign of Nebuchadnezzar, king of Babylon. Esther was born in captivity; this was all she knew. Although her beginning was as the humblest of figures, in four years she would become the queen of Persia. Mordecai loved Esther as his daughter.

The setting where Esther's story took place was the lavish palace of the Persian Empire. She became King Ahasuerus's wife (known as Xerxes I, reigning from 485–464 BC) after Vashti was deposed of her title and role as queen because she refused to be put on display before a drunken group of the king's friends. A few commentaries indicate that the request may have been for her to appear nude. Josephus records, "But she, out of regard for to the laws of Persians, which forbid wives to be seen by strangers, did not go to the king."[12] If this was the case, Vashti was a respectable woman of nobility and honor to refuse an unjust command of the king.

Haman would be a key figure in Esther's life as well. By birth, he was an Amalekite and still held resentment against the Jews because they had destroyed the Amalekite nation. Modern Jewish writers have described him as one whose behavior and hatred of the Jews was like Adolf Hitler. He had the ear of the king; in a modern-day setting, he would have been a prime minister.

After Vashti had been stripped of her title and position, King Ahasuerus ordered a search for a new queen. Esther, being a beautiful young lady, encouraged by Mordecai, was one of the women brought into the

12 William Whiston, *The Works of Josephus* (Peabody, MA: Hendrickson Publishers, 1987), 126.

harem. Mordecai warned her not to share that she was Jewish. According to Persian law, Esther's marriage was unlawful, which held that one from the royal line must marry someone belonging to the seven great Persian families. Curiously, no one around the king questioned who this girl was and where she came from. God strategically places his people to influence the future.

Hegai was one of the king's eunuchs in charge of the process of preparing the young virgins. He became fond of Esther and granted her special treatment. "She pleased him and won his favor. Immediately he provided her with her beauty treatments and special food. He assigned to her seven female attendants selected from the king's palace and moved her and her attendants into the best place in the harem" (Esther 2:9). Before these young ladies could go before the king, they had to go through twelve months of extensive beauty treatments.

Esther was smart and intuitive. When it was her time to go before the king, she sought Hegai's advice. She only asked for what Hegai suggested and won the favor of the king. Being so enamored with Esther, the king set the royal crown on her head and made her queen. He proclaimed a holiday in honor of the marriage.

Mordecai was always at the palace, keeping a watch over his charge. One day he overheard a plot to kill the king. "During the time Mordecai was sitting at the king's gate, Bigthana and Teresh, two of the king's officers who guarded the doorway, became angry and conspired to assassinate King Xerxes. But Mordecai found out about the plot and told Queen Esther, who in turn reported it to the king, giving credit to Mordecai" (Esther 2:21–22). The two men were executed, and the king recorded the account in the royal record. Again, we see God had positioned Esther and Mordecai in the right place to gain more and more favor while becoming more influential.

Haman's hatred for the Jews began to grow, especially toward Mordecai, who would not bow to him. The king had recently elevated Haman to a place of honor higher than any other nobles, and still, Mordecai refused to bow. Haman used his influence with the king to plot the genocide of the Jews. Haman cast a lot, and it came up the thirteenth day of the twelfth month for the destruction to begin. Mordecai sent word to Esther via one of her attendants: "Mordecai told him everything that had happened to him, including the exact amount of money Haman had promised to pay into the royal treasury for the destruction of the Jews. He also gave him a copy of the text of the edict for their annihilation, which had been published in Susa, to show to Esther and explain it to her, and he told him to instruct her to go into the king's presence to beg for mercy and plead with him for her people" (Esther 4:7–8).

When Esther first received word of this edict from Mordecai, her response was not what he had expected or hoped for. While she stayed in contact with her cousin, she also lived a life far removed from her Jewish kin. What exactly did he want her to do about it? "For any man or woman who approaches the king in the inner court without being summoned the king has but one law: that they be put to death unless the king extends the gold scepter to them and spares their lives" (Esther 4:11).

Esther's response was focused on her safety, and her lack of concern showed her disconnect. Fear of personal repercussions and being disconnected from matters that distress others can lead us to make hasty decisions that do not represent our Christian values. When one hurts, we all should feel the pain, show empathy, and express concern for that person's suffering. It is easy to make excuses because you can't help others; some are valid. But often, it is simply inconvenient. Helping others can be messy; you don't always have the time. As believers, we are called to get dirty if necessary, sacrifice on our day off, and possibly drive five miles in the other direction. Pray for more compassion toward the needs of others.

When Mordecai received Esther's response, he quoted words that have been used down through the ages to encourage, challenge, and convict people into participation and service: "Do not think that because you are in the king's house you alone of all the Jews will escape. For if you remain silent at this time, relief and deliverance for the Jews will arise from another place, but you and your father's family will perish. And who knows but that you have come to your royal position for such a time as this?" (Esther 4:13–14). Each of us has been placed in a particular location, ministry assignment, conflict, or position to effect change. The reason you are there may have appeared unorthodox as it unfolded. You questioned how and why, and so did others. As time went on and things began to unfold, it became clear that the responsibility to act had fallen to you.

Yes, God has all power. He can choose another if that is the answer. But the fact of the matter is that he has chosen *you*. If we survey the situation, we often find that we have been uniquely equipped for this moment. There was providential placing of Esther in the palace; she had been preordained to join God in this work.

Haman had created a groundswell of hatred toward the Jews and used his government position to make it law. Esther's assignment was great, and it could not be accomplished alone. She may have been the person out front, but she recognized that she was part of a greater community of people. She was willing to die for the cause, which was admirable; however, what I find more noteworthy is her courage to step out of the shadows. Kingdom impact takes courage and the mind of Christ that says, "Your will be done, on earth as it is in heaven" (Matthew 6:10).

Reflection

Esther had found favor with the king and those in the palace. I am sure most days, she did not dwell on the plight of the Jews, not because she was selfish but because it was no longer her world. Years had passed since she had become queen, and she had responsibilities in the role. The people loved her, so she was effective. By the time Mordecai sent word regarding the Jews' struggle, their problems were no longer her problems.

Success and upward mobility can sometimes cause us to forget the tough times. Now that we have more than our parents and have provided more for our children than what our parents dreamt for us, we can be disconnected from our nation's food insecurity. We have health care, so it's hard to imagine the millions of people turned away daily because they are without coverage. Poverty is what we witness on the news, but it is not present in the neighborhood where we live.

Mordecai's words *penetrated* Esther's heart. They reminded her of where she came from, lest she had forgotten. His words touched the innermost parts of her being. To make an impact in your community, you must be able to share in others' suffering. When Jesus encountered the suffering of people, he was "moved with compassion" (Matthew 9:36, NKJV). He was not moved *by* but *with* compassion. If we are moved *by* something, there will be limitations. To be moved *with* is to come alongside. Our compassion for another should join us to that person or cause.

In chapter four, I mentioned the birth of Priscilla's Lost and Found. This ministry was formed as the result of an encounter I had with a ten-year-old child. I had shared my testimony, and he was in the audience. The next Sunday, he approached me at church regarding his mother. She and I had similar stories, but she had yet to be delivered. He said to me, "Sister Arnetta, the Lord told me you would help my mother."

I did not meet his mother right away. Actually, I avoided this child for several weeks. I didn't want to get involved. I had several reasons why, but they were all excuses! Finally, I agreed. Immediately upon meeting this lady, my heart melted. I didn't see the sin; I saw her and was moved with compassion. Our relationship taught me so much about myself and about the heart of God. The connection grew into a strong friendship that we hold even today. The mission statement of Priscilla's Lost and Found was simple: *To use the model of Jesus to mentor and encourage women to achieve both spiritual and personal success.*

Compassion means that someone else's heartbreak becomes your heartbreak, and you are moved to action. If we see someone struggling or having a bad time, will we come alongside and help? May we be filled with an overwhelming desire to alleviate suffering in our communities. Pray that you can no longer pass the homeless, helpless, crack houses, and prostitutes without their needs tugging at your heart. Stop being concerned about how they got there and focus on what it takes to help get them out of there. Luke 6:36 (NLT) says, "You must be compassionate, just as your Father is compassionate."

Esther's compassion moved her to action. She called for reinforcements; she sought *partners* in her efforts to bring change. Esther called for a fast among the Jews. This fast is now known as Purim, which in English means "the Feast of the Lots." This joyous Jewish holiday continues to be celebrated today. It commemorates the survival of the Jews, who were marked for death by the Persian ruler's edict. During this commemoration, Jews may exchange gifts and often make donations to the poor. Even as they remember during this celebration, the desire to make an impact on the community is still present.

There is value in seeking collaboration and cooperation with fellow believers. We need one another. Throughout the Bible, God has called us into community. Yes, he clearly used the gifts of individuals, but when you look closely at the stories, seldom were they alone. Adam had Eve; Moses had Aaron; Deborah had Jael; Mary had Elizabeth; Paul had Silas. Over in the New Testament, Jesus instructed his disciples to go together: "Calling the Twelve to him, he began to send them out two by two and gave them authority over impure spirits" (Mark 6:7).

Esther and Mordecai were faced with the annihilation of their people. These may not be choices we face today, but we are called to respond for *such a time as this* in our own communities. What are we doing together to advance the kingdom of God? We are called to work together for the common good. There is a greater impact on our communities when we participate in Kingdom-empowered collaborations.

There is added impact when people work together. Co-laboring brings a good return and is an indicator of a Spirit-filled church. We accomplish so much more when we have someone to help us. We were not created by God to live in a vacuum. I remember reading years ago that no one accomplishes success alone. Every successful person had someone to encourage and advise him or her along the way. Even if what this person was doing was radical and the naysayers outnumbered the supporters, it was the voice of the encouragers that he or she listened to. All of us need colleagues in ministry.

God doesn't ask you to do anything you are not equipped to handle. Don't move before your time; *prepare*.

I remember when God began to speak to me about the ministry of Priscilla's Lost and Found. I was so excited; I couldn't wait to go and tell folks what I wanted to do. Boy, was I disappointed with the reception. People looked at me strangely, and very few joined in my joy. I went back to God, dejected, ready to give up before I even began. What I would later discover in my haste was my lack of planning and clarity of purpose.

I went back to God and entered a season of prayer and fasting. When I presented my idea again, I received overwhelming support. The Lord blessed me with words of encouragement from key leaders to move forward and monetary gifts to begin the work.

Esther had a plan, but she recognized it would take time and care to bring to execution. Had she presented her thoughts prematurely to the king inside the court, Haman would have found out. She was patient, wise, and diplomatic in the execution of her plan.

The story of Esther does not end here. She executed her plan well. The destruction Haman had planned for the Jews became his death sentence. "In him we were also chosen, having been predestined according to the plan of him who works out everything in conformity with the purpose of his will" (Ephesians 1:11).

Conclusion

When we encounter so much hate, destruction, pain, and hopelessness around us, we wonder where God is. He is there, fully engaged. The Book of Esther never mentions God, yet we see his hand at work. His timing was impeccable, and his placement for those who would assist him was creative. Look for God among those who may never mention him by name. He has placed you among them to be the light.

Statements of Truth

1. God will use you if you are willing; he will make you capable.
2. Handicaps and adversities do not affect what God has ordained for you to accomplish.
3. God puts you where he wants to fulfill your mission in life.
4. We have been placed in a position to show compassion and advocate for those who are in need.

CHAPTER 12

Global Impact

He said to them "Go into all the world and preach the gospel to all creation".... Then the disciples went out and preached everywhere, and the Lord worked with them and confirmed his word by the signs that accompanied it. —Mark 16:15, 20

I love the clarity of Jesus' command. He does not give room for us to ask the questions "How far?" and "To whom?" Everywhere and everyone!

God knows who we are; he is keenly aware of our weaknesses as well as our strengths. His command for us to live out the Great Commission is not based on our own abilities, yet it can be strengthened by our personal experiences. When the disciples followed Jesus' command they were successful, not because they were perfect but because he was with them. Christ's Spirit is actively at work in our lives. When we are under the influence of the Holy Spirit and are willing to share our authentic testimony with others, we have power.

Jesus was speaking to his disciples. The conversation was being held right after the resurrection and before his ascension to heaven. For three years he had been preparing them for this moment. He had called each one of them individually; he dealt with them personally. Yes, there were group lessons, but he also took the time to provide one-on-one teaching opportunities for growth coaching. For example, Jesus spoke to Thomas's doubting spirit after the resurrection: "Because you have seen me, you have believed; blessed are those who have not seen and yet have believed" (John 20:29).

When James and John wanted Jesus to call down fire to destroy a village, Jesus rebuked them. Right after Jesus had performed the great miracle of feeding the five thousand, Peter showed a lack of faith whether he could walk on water at Jesus' invitation: "Immediately Jesus reached out his hand and caught him. 'You of little faith,' he said, 'why did you doubt?' " (Matthew 14:31). Remember, these men—Peter, James, and John—made up Jesus' inner circle, yet this did not prohibit them from being corrected when necessary.

You may never travel to the continent of Africa or Asia or witness the ice-covered mountains of Elephant Island in Antarctica, but if there truly is a six-degree separation from connecting with everyone on this planet, your witness matters. How you live out your faith in the grocery store can reach the hearts of your neighbor in the Spanish Islands. Why not take a chance and ask God to give you a "go ye" moment—one in which age, location, or circumstance will not define your ability? This moment can turn into a lifestyle, and your living witness will have a lasting impact throughout eternity.

Jesus promised to be with us. His presence will override any differences that stand in the way. May we decide to be participants rather than onlookers. Go ye into the suburbs of your hometown—that is your Jerusalem. Samaria is your community, and "to the ends of the earth" is all nations. Friends, we can change the world right where we live, work, and play. You never know whom you will encounter from the other end of the earth.

Mary of Bethany: A Witness for All Eternity

Luke 10:38–42; John 11:1–44

This Mary is often identified by her location of birth, as is Mary Magdalene. No other details regarding her origin are mentioned in the Scriptures. Bethany was located on the east side of the Mount of Olives, beside the Jericho Road, two miles to the east of Jerusalem. Jesus went to Bethany on several occasions, especially for a visit with Mary's family, whom he had a great fondness for.

Mary was the sister of Martha and Lazarus. The home in which they lived was owned by Martha. Much has been written about the contrasting personalities of these sisters. Martha was a woman of hospitality and made her home welcoming to Jesus. Mary was quieter and more reserved. Lazarus was loved by Jesus; when he became ill, word was sent to Jesus: "Lord, the one you love is sick" (John 11:3).

There is never any mention of Jesus returning to his childhood home, but there are several occasions where he was said to be in the home of this family. This is the first mention of the family in Scripture. The opening adjective describes the personalities and position of these two sisters. It was Martha's home, but it was Mary's moment. As Luke tells the story, his choice of words leaves nothing to the imagination. Martha was distracted; she was not focused on what was right or relevant—Jesus. In our quest to be witnesses, we must never miss an opportunity to be in the presence of the Lord. He was there with them in person; we have him with us in Spirit every day. Are we so preoccupied with the mundane that we miss the Master?

Mary is mentioned four distinct times in the biblical text. However, it is important to draw attention to the fact that every time she was in the presence of Jesus, she was at his feet. To sit at someone's feet is a sign of confidence in that person, a willingness to learn from what he or she has to say. You expect guidance and accept this person's direction humbly.

"As Jesus and his disciples were on their way, he came to a village where a woman named Martha opened her home to him. She had a sister called Mary, who sat at the Lord's feet listening to what he said. But Martha was distracted by all the preparations that had to be made. She came to him and asked, 'Lord, don't you care that my sister has left me to do the work by myself? Tell her to help me!' 'Martha, Martha,' the Lord answered, 'you are worried and upset about many things, but few things are needed—or indeed only one. Mary has chosen what is better, and it will not be taken away from her' " (Luke 10:38–42). Mary was confident in who she was and comfortable with her choices. She never tried to defend herself or justify her actions during criticism or when mocked by another, specifically where her faith was concerned.

Mary could have countered with an explanation or a justification for why she was not assisting Martha. Here is a good example of knowing when to speak and when to stay silent; when in the service of Lord, trust him to be your advocate. When we are doing the right thing, making the right choices, he will reward, keep, and sustain us. He is our defender. "Vindicate me, LORD, for I have led a blameless life; I have trusted in the LORD and have not faltered" (Psalm 26:1). Mary focused; her time with Jesus was more important that day than the chores.

Some commentaries call Mary a spiritual scholar. "Usually the rabbis, or teachers, sit on a high chair, and their scholars on the ground, and so they are literally at their master's feet. This was Mary's position as with all teachableness she hearkened to the Lord."[13] We cannot let the cares of life interrupt our time with God. Mary would not be denied her time. Whatever activity draws your focus draws you away from the Lord. Martha complained to Jesus that Mary was shirking her duties.

Mary's next encounter with Jesus was on a very sad day. "When Mary reached the place where Jesus was and saw him, she fell at his feet and said, 'Lord, if you had been here, my brother would not have died.' When Jesus saw her weeping, and the Jews who had come along with her also weeping, he was deeply moved in spirit and troubled" (John 11:32–33).

Mary and Martha had sent for Jesus because Lazarus was sick. Jesus had loved Lazarus; everyone knew that, even the disciples. I am sure everyone expected him to respond right away, to rush to his friend. However, Jesus stayed where he was two more days. There is much in this narrative that seems to be contradictory, but everything that was done aligned itself to bring glory to God, strengthen the faith of the believers, and silence the naysayers.

---

13 Herbert Lockyer, *All the Women of the Bible* (Grand Rapids, MI: Zondervan Corporation, 1967), 105.

Jesus declared, "This sickness will not end in death" (v 4), but he knew Lazarus would initially die. When Martha heard that Jesus was coming, she went quickly to meet him, but Mary stayed home. Both sisters were grieving the loss of their brother, one more pensive and the other impulsive. Martha said to Jesus, "If you had been here, my brother would not have died" (v 21). Martha's exchange with Jesus was powerful and would become a prophetic accounting for the miracle of his own resurrection. "I am the resurrection and the life. The one who believes in me will live, even though they die; and whoever lives by believing in me will never die. Do you believe this?" (vv 25–26). Martha's faith was on full display in her response: " 'Yes, Lord,' she replied, 'I believe that you are the Messiah, the Son of God, who is to come into the world' " (v 27).

Scripture does not record Jesus' request, but apparently he asked for Mary. When Mary arrived with those who were with her for comfort, she fell at his feet and wept. Jesus was "deeply moved in spirit and troubled" (v 33). Mary's tears, and those of the Jews who accompanied her, touched the heart of Jesus. He was also troubled. Could it be that he was troubled because he could see that there were some in the crowd who were simply spectators, standing ready to accuse him for his actions? Whatever it was, Jesus displayed public sorrow for his friend: "Jesus wept" (v 35).

Mary's admiration and love toward Jesus was not overridden by her sorrow. She still fell at his feet. He was still her master, and she had confidence in him. Mary did not understand Jesus' delay, just as Martha had not, but her posture was different. She came as one whose actions said *I submit to your will.*

Trust God through your grief; he will free you from emotions that cripple, feelings that paralyze, thoughts of anger, and grudges or actions that destroy your well-being. What you are going though or went through has not been in vain. Your season of anguish "will not end in death" (v 4). Jesus can and will resurrect those things that appear to be dead or dying. Draw closer to him; in his presence, sufferings become lighter and broken hearts are mended. Don't alienate yourself, come nearer. Your pain and sorrow have touched the heart of God.

We often end the story of Lazarus being raised from the dead with the loosing of the grave clothes, but that was not the last of the action. Mary's influence continued: "Therefore many of the Jews who had come to visit Mary, and had seen what Jesus did, believed in him" (v 45). There are people who will come to know Jesus because of what they have seen in your life. You are someone's miracle. When your problem seemed insurmountable, someone was watching how you navigated those times. People will respond to your level of faith and your trust in God that never ceased. Our impact can be great even when we have no idea that people are watching, looking silently at our living witness.

Mary's final time with Jesus as recorded in the Scriptures was, "While [Jesus] was in Bethany, reclining at the table in the home of Simon the Leper, a woman came with an alabaster jar of very expensive perfume, made of pure nard. She broke the jar and poured the perfume on his head. Some of those present were saying indignantly to one another, 'Why this waste of perfume? It could have been sold for more than a year's wages and the money given to the poor.' And they rebuked her harshly. 'Leave her alone,' said Jesus. 'Why are you bothering her? She has done a beautiful thing to me. The poor you will always have with you, and you can help them any time you want. But you will not always have me. She did what she could. She poured perfume on my body beforehand to prepare for my burial. Truly I tell you, wherever the gospel is preached throughout the world, what she has done will also be told, in memory of her' " (Mark 14:3–9).

John 12 recounts this same story and calls Mary by name. Often this story has been confused with the woman who was a sinner in Luke 7:36–50. The stories are similar, but they are different women.

John's account tells us that a dinner was given in honor of Jesus. Mary and Martha were there in gratitude for what Jesus had done for Lazarus; many of the other guests were probably there out of curiosity. Martha again was serving. Mary knelt again at Jesus' feet and began to anoint them with expensive perfume. Judas Iscariot was indignant and complained about the cost. A year's wages were worth three hundred denarii, a significant sum in that day. Jesus again spoke on Mary's behalf, "Leave her alone" (v 7). In Mark 14:8 he said, "She did what she could."

If you love this story as much as I do, this statement is life giving. Every time I read it, it is as though I am reading it again for the first time. This text affirms that my ordinary efforts in God's service are extraordinary. All my thoughts of being less-than and insecure are canceled by who God says I am.

Mary did not lead an army into battle like Deborah or boldly stand before King David in an effort to save her family from destruction like Abigail. She was not a church planter comparable to Priscilla or a businesswoman like Lydia. She poured oil. How much talent was on display to pour oil? She "did what she could"; she offered to Jesus what she had. Honor was not given to her for being a great preacher, excellent teacher, psalmist, or musician. She poured oil from an alabaster jar.

Now, I hope someone just laid this book down and began to shout. This chapter is about impact. It is about having influence, power, the ability to sway others, being a force to be reckoned with. Here is my paraphrase of what Jesus said in defense of Mary: "Stop, wait a minute! Here is the model, the example to follow. All that you have done or failed to do when I came into your presence has paled in comparison to what she did."

Jesus memorialized Mary for all of eternity. If her action had impact on Christ, if it caused him to stop and take notice, surely there is a lesson to be learned for all of us. Free yourself from judging and comparing what you have to offer against what another person brings. Just bring your best. If we are willing to pour out our gifts, no matter what they are, into the lives of others, a life will be changed. From one generation to the next, someone will recall what Mary did. The same is true for you and me. Someone will recall our life and our deed, how our simple gift was amazingly powerful, how it moved the hearts of people because we humbly gave what we had.

Reflection
How tough of a journey it had to be for Mary to live a life of constantly being misunderstood. One could understand if she took on the posture of being a victim, if she were always ready to defend herself, walked around with a chip on her shoulder, or just simply said, "Forget it. I am tired of trying to please everyone, I will just give up." I am so glad Mary kept going; her quiet nature spoke volumes. One might ask, "Is this the personality of a world changer?"

Well, let us ask Mother Teresa, winner of the Nobel Peace Prize for caring for the sick and poor. She founded the Missionaries of Charity as a result of a second calling from God while riding on a train in India. He instructed her to abandon teaching and work in the slums of Calcutta. She faced criticism and self-doubt, but every day she did what she could. She was quoted as saying, "If you can't feed a hundred people, feed just one." Millions of lives were changed for good because of this gentle servant of God.

Let's ask those who knew Dr. Mary McLeod Bethune. Was she a world changer? Wherever Dr. Bethune saw a need, she found a way to meet that need and move society closer to her vision. She opened a hospital in Daytona Beach to serve the Black community. When the nation mobilized resources for the first and second World Wars, she pressed for the integration of the American Red Cross and Women's Army Auxiliary Corps. She relied on her faith in God. Without faith, nothing is possible. With it, nothing is impossible. [14]

Many have criticized Martha for her desire to have Mary help in the kitchen. Although we are living in the twenty-first century, there are still things that are often relegated as women's work. There are those who still expect women to perform in these areas alone. Yes, the glass ceiling is shattering across our nation and around the world. In recent times we have seen the election of our first woman as Vice President of the United States. This has even more significance because she is a woman of color. However, I would like to note that even in the patriarchal world of the Bible there were women of color leading nations. The queen of Sheba, visitor to King Solomon in 1 Kings 10:1–13, was an Ethiopian. Jesus referenced her in Luke 11:31 as "the Queen of the South." Pharoah's daughter, who fetched Moses from the river in Exodus 2:5–7, was an Egyptian princess.

God never intended for there to be a ceiling, which is why it was made of glass. It is meant to be shattered!

Mary embraced being a *unique* creation as exemplified in Psalm 139:14, "I praise you because I am fearfully and wonderfully made." She was not trying to live up to anyone's definition of who she was other than being a follower of Christ. She went against the norm of the day, which is exactly what Jesus was doing. He was breaking down walls of separation. He was elevating women in ways that had not been done before. May we learn to celebrate more the uniqueness found in one another and give space for diversity and distinctiveness.

My sister, we are each one of a kind. When God created us, he set us apart and prescribed something different for each one of us to do. When

14 Adapted from "Our Founder - Dr. Bethune," accessed April 5, 2021, https://www.cookman.edu/about_BCU/history/our_founder.html.

we became followers of Christ, he endowed each of us with spiritual gifts and abilities. Mary was willing to sacrifice her popularity to discover her personhood. Be well with what God has given you. Martha was great at what she was doing; it's too bad she couldn't see that too many cooks in the kitchen spoils the meal. She had the gift of hospitality, and Mary had other gifts—she was an encourager to Jesus.

I remember my first peaching class. We had to write three sermons during the semester, but the final activity was to preach for fifteen minutes. I received a *C* on all three written sermons. The grade bothered me, but the comments confused me even more. The professor criticized everything! There were so many red marks and comments in the margins of my paper that you could barely see what I had written. I went to him several times, trying to understand what I was doing wrong. To no avail, my grade never changed. I had resolved that the most I would get from this class was a *C*, which his notes implied had been generous.

On the day I was to preach one of the sermons submitted during the semester, I chose the sermon with the least number of red marks. I stood before the class with butterflies in my stomach but determined to preach what I believed was a word from God. However, still in the back of my mind were the thoughts of his grading my inadequacies. Upon completion, the professor asked that I stay after class. He apologized profusely for my past grades. His comment was, "I didn't understand your *style*; it is non-traditional. After listening to you, I am compelled to change your grade and to rethink how I teach this class."

God created us each to be different, yet to have commonalities. We were made in his image and his likeness. But each one of us has our own personality, temperament, style, and distinct experiences. Mary was certain of what she was called to do: sit at the feet of Jesus. Understanding what makes you unique will help you better know what you have to offer. Knowing yourself will help guide you on the path to the best ways God wants to use you to share the gospel.

Martha was a go-getter; she made things happen and ran immediately to Jesus when she heard he was coming. Mary stayed at home. Mary's posture in staying home appeared to be *unassertive*. One could think that she was detached or passive. But it is not a weakness to show meekness. Everyone is different, and assertive is not the only recommended trait. How would we get anything accomplished if everyone was forceful and insistent? Yet, even those with more assertive personalities have balanced this trait at times, knowing when it is more productive to be retiring.

Some theologians theorize that Mary was emotionally fragile, and her grief had immobilized her. When people do not understand you, they will often label you incorrectly. Mary was far from being immobile; she was waiting for Jesus.

As the years have progressed, I have become more assertive, but it is an uncomfortable place for me. I am an introvert by nature who has had to learn to live, function, and serve in an extroverted world. I am more comfortable living in the background. Often I have been underestimated and looked over because of my failure to speak up.

I come from a family of preachers, pastors, church planters, and siblings who always seemed to know what they wanted and how to achieve it. They are yesterday, today, and always my heroes. I remember one of the most precious moments in my life was the day I preached my first sermon and my dad, Elder Dr. Timmie McNeese, introduced me. To this day, I wish his intro had been recorded because it was an apt description of my life up to that point. His description was loving, thought provoking, and a clear picture of the power of God in one's life.

When my dad stood to introduce me, he began to tell the story of Jesse and David. He equated it to his children. He kept waiting for the Lord to call one of his children into ministry, but it never happened. He kept looking and asking God, "Is it this one?" But each time, he said, the oil would not run. When I called early one Sunday morning to tell him I had accepted my call to the ministry, the oil ran. The Lord had called the last child, the one whom no one would ever imagine it to be. Praise God, my dad's prayers have been answered again and again. During the ten years after I received my call, four more of his children answered their call to ministry.

Mild-mannered Mary, the one who never spoke up other than this one time when Lazarus had died, touched the heart of Jesus time after time by her actions more than her words. Mary lived her truth, the person God created her to be, with no pretense. Live your truth; you are the best of God's creation. "Before I formed you in the womb I knew you, before you were born I set you apart" (Jeremiah 1:5).

Usually when you hear the words *She did what she could*, they are not followed by great expectations. You imagine the extra work needed to modify or fix what's been done. This declaration is not a statement of finality. But when Jesus spoke these words, there was nothing else needed, nothing else to be said. The task was complete, a job well done.

Mary's gratefulness, love, and adoration for Jesus were all bottled in that alabaster jar. She poured her appreciation and admiration on the one who accepted her just as she was and never *underestimated* what she had to offer. The value of the oil was not in the price; it was her relationship with Jesus that was priceless.

Conclusion

God will use the simplicity of who we are and what we bring to him to do extraordinary things for the kingdom. Stop trying to fix the things that make you unique. I am not saying to overlook self-improvement, but cease feeling as though you are not enough. You are. You are just who God envisioned when he created you.

Be the light, one who is not ashamed of the gospel of Christ. When we allow the gospel to impact our lives, our witness becomes brighter. Imagine how many souls you can reach for the Kingdom if you do what you can while you can as much as you can for as long as you can.

Don't underestimate the power of your witness!

Questions for Reflection

1. Do you see yourself as a global influencer? If not, why?
2. Who are the influencers in your life? What is it that makes them influencers?
3. How can you prevent your sorrow from impeding you from sharing the gospel?

CPSIA information can be obtained
at www.ICGtesting.com
Printed in the USA
BVHW051230270721
612359BV00004B/6